T0294276

CHARLES
DICKENS

Series Editor C.S. Nicholls

Highly readable brief lives of those who have played a significant part in history, and whose contributions still influence contemporary culture.

CHARLES DICKENS

CATHERINE PETERS

First published 1998
This edition first published 2009

The History Press
The Mill, Brimscombe Port
Stroud, Gloucestershire, GL5 2QG
www.thehistorypress.co.uk

British Library Cataloguing in Publication Data.
A catalogue record for this book is available from the British Library.

ISBN 978 0 7524 5226 5

Typesetting and origination by The History Press
Printed in Great Britain

C O N T E N T S

A CKNOWLEDGEMENT

I am most grateful to the editor-in-chief, Graham Storey, and the Oxford University Press, for permission to quote extensively from the magnificent *Pilgrim Edition of the Letters of Charles Dickens*.

CHRONOLOGY

1812	**7 February.** Born at 13 Mile End Terrace, Landport, Portsmouth
1817	Family move to Chatham, Kent
1822	Family move to London. Dickens not sent to school
1824	**9 February.** Begins work in Warren's blacking warehouse. Father imprisoned for debt
	June. Dickens sent to Wellington House Academy
1827	Leaves school, begins work as a solicitor's clerk
1830	Meets and becomes engaged to Maria Beadnell
1831	Becomes parliamentary shorthand reporter
1834	Begins to publish 'Sketches', using the pseudonym 'Boz'
1836	*Sketches by Boz*. Marries Catherine Hogarth
1837	*Pickwick Papers*. Birth of Charles Dickens jnr. Death of Catherine's sister Mary
1838	*Oliver Twist*. Birth of Mary (Mamie) Dickens
1839	*Nicholas Nickleby*. Birth of Kate Dickens
1841	*Old Curiosity Shop, Barnaby Rudge*. Birth of Walter Dickens
1842	**Jan/June.** Visits America. *American Notes*. Georgina Hogarth joins the Dickens household

1843	*A Christmas Carol*
1844	*Martin Chuzzlewit*. Birth of Francis Dickens **from July.** living in Italy
1845	*The Cricket on the Hearth*. Directs and acts in *Every Man in his Humour*. Birth of Alfred Dickens
1846	*Pictures from Italy, The Battle of Life*. Living in Lausanne and Paris
1847	Involvement with Urania Cottage. Birth of Sydney Dickens
1848	*Dombey and Son*. Death of Dickens's sister Fanny
1849	Birth of Henry Dickens
1850	*David Copperfield. Household Words* begins publication. Birth of Dora Dickens
1851	Deaths of Dickens's father and daughter Dora
1852	Birth of Edward (Plorn) Dickens
1853	*Bleak House.* Gives first public reading, of *A Christmas Carol*
1854	*Hard Times*
1855	Directs and acts in *The Lighthouse*, by Wilkie Collins. Living in Paris for some months
1856	Buys Gad's Hill Place
1857	*Little Dorrit*. Directs and acts in *The Frozen Deep*. Meets Nelly Ternan
1858	Separates from his wife. Begins professional readings from his works
1859	*A Tale of Two Cities. All the Year Round* begins publication
1861	*Great Expectations*

Chronology

1865	*Our Mutual Friend*. Involved in Staplehurst railway accident, with Nelly Ternan
1867	**November.** Begins reading tour of America, which ends in May 1868
1868	Farewell reading tour cut short when Dickens has a slight stroke
1870	**March.** Last public reading, *A Christmas Carol*. Starts *The Mystery of Edwin Drood*
	9 June. dies leaving *Drood* unfinished. Buried in Westminster Abbey

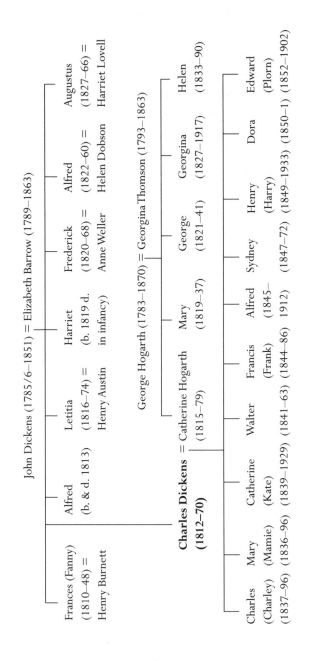

Charles Dickens's family tree.

INTRODUCTION

In the summer of 1841 Edinburgh greeted a hero: the 29-year-old Charles Dickens. He was given the freedom of the city. Over 250 male guests attended one of several dinners held in his honour, with nearly as many women looking on from a gallery. When he went to the theatre, the audience, warned by the newspapers that 'Boz' would be present, crammed in to see him. As he entered, the orchestra struck up 'Charley is my Darling'.

This extraordinary popularity lasted his whole life. Dickens's creative genius was fully recognized, not by a select readership but by a mass audience. He was read by rich and poor, the newly literate and the highly educated: 'almost everybody whose letters and biography have come down to us has something to say about Dickens'.[1] What was the secret of his success?

He was of course a great entertainer, who could move from drama to comedy in a sentence, arousing the emotions and engaging the sympathies of his readers. But he was concerned with the major issues of his times, and his criticisms, many of them still valid today, challenged his readers' consciences and intelligence. Dickens saw astonishing changes; during his lifetime Britain was transformed from a predominantly rural economy to a major industrial power. Transport, mass communications, education, legal and parliamentary structures, the treatment of the insane and criminals, the position of women, were all radically altered. Because of Dickens's immense popularity, he had an influence on the shaping of social policy. Politicians read him, and knew they had to take account of what he wrote.

If Dickens's novels were merely melodrama or fictionalized social commentary we should not read them today. He also had the gift of imaginative insight, a playwright's ear for dialogue and, above all, an ability to sum up a scene or a character in a wholly original but startlingly exact image. It is this invention and humour, the eye for the bizarre poetry of everyday life, which makes his writing live. His responses did not remain static. There are differences between his picaresque early novels, the increased complexity of his major middle period, and the dark intensity of his later work. But whether he is being funny or terrifying, realistic or wildly improbable, the energy of the writing remains compelling. The 'Dickens world' he created is like no other.

Dickens was not only a novelist. In his fifty-eight years he accomplished as much as three or four people combined. He wrote penetrating, investigative journalism. He was a meticulous editor who personally read and revised the contributions to his magazines, a talented amateur actor and a magnificent reader from his own work. He played an active part in charitable enterprises and welfare schemes. He walked 10 or 15 miles a day. Over 14,000 letters written in his own hand, some of them many pages long, are known to have survived: many more have disappeared.

A brief biography can give only a flavour of Dickens. As he wrote to a critic of his novel *Barnaby Rudge*, 'the object is – not to tell everything, but to select the striking points and beat them into the page with a sledge-hammer'.[2] There are many excellent biographies and critical appraisals of his work, some of them listed in the bibliography. Best of all, read Dickens himself. His novels have been a source of delight to me since I was ten years old. I shall go on reading them until I die.

CHILDHOOD AND YOUTH, 1812−32

harles Dickens was born at 13 Mile End Terrace, Landport, Portsmouth, on 7 February 1812, into a young, cheerful and improvident household. He was the second child and eldest son of John Dickens, a clerk in the Navy Pay Office, and his wife Elizabeth, a pretty, vain 23-year-old, rumoured to have been dancing at a ball shortly before her son's birth.

John Dickens's parents had been upper servants in the household of Lord Crewe. His father, the steward, died when John was ten. His mother rose to be housekeeper and was immortalized by her grandson as the stately Mrs Rouncewell in *Bleak House*. John Dickens had a disastrous fondness for a gentlemanly style of living, which was perhaps inspired by the great houses he had known from below stairs as a child. His wife's family, the Barrows, belonged to the middle class to which he aspired, but they were haunted by a financial scandal. In 1810 Elizabeth's father, also employed in the Navy Pay Office, was caught embezzling large amounts of money, and fled to the Continent to escape imprisonment.

John and Elizabeth Dickens soon proved to be losers in the battle of life, and Charles grew up in the shabby-genteel world he was often to describe in his fiction. There were no safety nets for failures, and children from such a background learnt early the value of self-presentation. A few became great actors and great writers; many more, the hypocrites and confidence tricksters Dickens drew in his novels. His early experiences provided rich material for his writing, but also left him with a hatred of the 'toadyism' and pretence produced by the English class system.

The Dickens family never settled anywhere for very long. Before Charles was six months old they were on the move, and before he was twelve had changed their living quarters eight times. His parents were often evicted for the non-payment of rent, or were 'flitting', desperately attempting to keep ahead of creditors. John Dickens was in perpetual financial trouble. His sanguine, easy-going temperament, which contrasted with brief fits of acute, even suicidal depression, are brilliantly captured in the character of Wilkins Micawber in *David Copperfield*. Waiting hopefully 'in case anything turned up'[1] even as he slid further and further into debt, John Dickens was constitutionally unable to live within his means.

Eight children, of whom six survived infancy, did not improve the situation. The eldest, Fanny, was born in 1810, Letitia, the only one of Charles Dickens's siblings to outlive him, in 1816. Frederick and Alfred arrived in 1820 and 1822. The youngest child, Augustus, was born after a gap of five years, in 1827. Charles and his sister Fanny, his elder by only fifteen months, were thus set apart by four and five years from the younger children, and their relationship was close and affectionate.

When Charles was five, the family moved to Chatham, Kent, where John Dickens was employed in the naval dockyard. It was a lively, bustling town, full of sailors and soldiers. To the north were the misty, sinister Kent marshes with the prison hulks moored off-shore, the setting for Pip's terrifying encounter with the convict Magwitch in the opening chapter of *Great Expectations*. A few miles to the west, a complete contrast to lively Chatham, lay the drowsy city of Rochester, with its ancient cathedral and castle, 'Cloisterham' in Dickens's last novel, *The Mystery of Edwin Drood*.

These were the most settled years of Charles's childhood, and they lived in his memory as a golden age. A rise in John Dickens's salary to £300 a year led to a period of relative stability, and though his income soon had to be buttressed by loans cadged from friends and relatives – more often used for entertaining than to pay the tradesmen's bills – the family lived in a comfortable house with a garden. Even then Charles may have been burdened by underlying insecurity, for he vividly remembered his bad dreams and childhood terrors.

Some were induced by his nurse, Mary Weller. Dickens recalled how she scared him out of his wits with bloodthirsty tales. Her combination of the stories of Bluebeard and Sweeney Todd in the tale of 'Captain Murderer' who baked his brides in a pie, was particularly horrific. He later believed it was his nurse who aroused his fascination with the dangerous edge of things. 'If we all knew our own minds (in a more enlarged sense than the popular acceptation of that phrase),' Dickens wrote, 'I suspect we should find our nurses responsible for most of the dark corners we are forced to go back to, against our own wills.'[2]

He was small in size, and not strong. He had attacks of feverish illness throughout his childhood, with pains in his side which persisted into adult life, and had not yet developed the immense physical energy he prided himself on later. Rather than joining in boys' games, he read voraciously. His father had acquired a cheap edition of standard novels, and before he was ten Charles was reading *Robinson Crusoe*, *The Arabian Nights*, *Don Quixote*, and the novels of Smollett and Fielding, visualizing the characters and acting out their stories until they became more real to him than the world around him.

He also started to write, first plays and then stories; his lifelong passion for the theatre was awoken at Chatham. He and his sister Fanny, a gifted musician, were often called on by their proud father to entertain visitors with recitations and comic songs, and Charles discovered that the imaginative world so vivid to him could be projected and made real to others. He was often taken to the Theatre Royal in Chatham by an army doctor, Dr Lamert. Lamert was courting his mother's widowed sister, who had lived with the Dickens family for most of Charles's early life. Charles remembered how 'Richard the Third, in a very uncomfortable cloak, . . . had made my heart leap with terror by backing up against the stage box in which I was posted, while struggling for life against the virtuous Richmond.'[3] When Dr Lamert married Charles's aunt and they moved to Ireland, his son James, a teenager who befriended the little boy, lodged with the Dickens family. He continued to take Charles to plays and later made him a toy theatre.

Formal education played a minor part in Dickens's childhood; when his father was later asked where his son had been educated, he replied, Micawber-like,

'Why, indeed, Sir – ha! ha! – he may be said to have educated himself!'[4] Charles was at first taught by his mother, as were most children at the time, and, like David Copperfield, recalled with pleasure 'the fat black letters in the primer, the puzzling novelty of their shapes, and the easy good-nature of O and Q and S'.[5] Next came a dame school of which he had only hazy memories.

By the summer of 1821 the spacious house had to be given up. A smaller one was found near the dockyard, and Charles and Fanny were sent to a school next door, run by a clergyman. Charles remembered Mr Giles with affection, though he felt the lessons were rather haphazard. A year later the precarious happiness of the Chatham years came to an end.

John Dickens was transferred to Somerset House, the London headquarters of the Navy Pay Office, with a reduction in his salary. Charles was left to board with Mr Giles for a few months, before being despatched to London, alone, in the stage-coach. He never forgot 'the smell of the damp straw in which I was packed – like game – and forwarded, carriage paid'.[6] He found the family settled in a mean house in Bayham Street, Camden Town, with a washerwoman as next-door neighbour. It was the beginning of the worst period of his life.

To his surprise he was not sent to school at the end of the summer, but kept at home to run errands and polish his father's boots, neglected and solitary. For the first time the full weight of his father's money problems became clear to the child. As they slipped into the direst poverty, he was despatched to sell or pawn the few remaining possessions of any value, including the precious books he had first read at Chatham. He later said of his father, 'he appeared to have utterly lost at this time the idea of educating me at all, and to have utterly put from him the notion that I had any claim upon him in that regard, whatever'.[7] Yet when the newly established Royal Academy of Music opened its doors to the first pupils the following spring, Fanny Dickens was sent there as a boarder, at a cost, that could ill be afforded, of 38 guineas a year. The contrast with Charles's own neglect was unbearably painful.

In a last forlorn attempt to avoid disaster the family moved in the autumn of 1823 to a house in Gower Street, where, with no experience or training, Elizabeth Dickens tried to start a school. A brass plate was screwed to the door; circulars were printed and Charles ordered to leave them at all the doors in the locality. Not surprisingly, there were no takers, and in this extremity James Lamert suggested a way for Charles to contribute to the household.

Lamert was working in the counting house of a blacking factory owned by his cousin. He arranged for Charles to be employed there, covering the pots of blacking with paper and pasting labels on them, at a wage of 6*s* a week. He began work there on 9 February 1824, two days after his twelfth birthday.

It was the crucial experience of his life. He could not later remember how long he had spent in the tumbledown factory, overrun with rats, on the river at Hungerford Stairs, Strand; his agony seemed to go on for ever. In fact, it seems to have been at most five months. The only company he had was his fellow-workers, illiterate boys with whom he had nothing in common, though they were kind to him in their rough way. He later wrote in a passage that went almost word for word into *David Copperfield*:

No words can express the secret agony of my soul as
I sunk into this companionship . . . and felt my early
hopes of growing up to be a learned and distinguished
man crushed in my breast . . . the sense I had of being
utterly neglected and hopeless; of the shame I felt in
my position; of the misery it was to my young heart to
believe that, day by day, what I had learned, and
thought, and delighted in . . . was passing away from
me, never to be brought back any more.[8]

The experience was to affect the whole course of his
life and work, and his campaigns on behalf of neglected
and abused children sprang from his own knowledge.
Many poor children began work at twelve, or younger,
in the 1820s, but Charles had been brought up with
middle-class expectations. From being a cherished and
admired eldest son, in a lively, if chaotic household, he
had now been abandoned as worthless. The few
shillings a week he earned barely served for his keep,
so that his sacrifice seemed gratuitous, a means of
getting him out of the way. It was a fairy story in
reverse; through no fault of his own the prince had
become a swineherd.

Ten days after Charles began work, John Dickens
was arrested for debt and imprisoned in the

Marshalsea, the debtors' prison. Elizabeth Dickens and the three younger children joined her husband in the prison, where, since John Dickens's salary continued to be paid, they were rather better off than before. They even kept the little maidservant from the Chatham workhouse who had come to London with them. Charles, however, was sent into lodgings in Camden Town with an old woman who later inspired the character of the formidable Mrs Pipchin in *Dombey and Son*.

Now the last vestiges of home life disappeared. His landlady did not provide his meals, and out of his 6*s* a week he had to budget for his breakfast and supper of bread, milk and cheese, as well as lunch. He found it hard to manage his money, and was often penniless and hungry at the week's end. 'No advice, no counsel, no encouragement, no consolation, no support, from any one that I can call to mind, so help me God.'[9] He wondered later why he had not become a little thief. He saw his family only on Sundays, when he collected Fanny from the Royal Academy and they spent the day at the prison. After a while he prevailed on his father to let him live nearer the prison, so that he could at least join the family for breakfast and supper.

John Dickens was released from prison at the end of May, under the Insolvent Debtors' Act. But there was no immediate release for his son. When he went to see his sister receive a silver medal at the Royal Academy he wept at the humiliation of his position compared with hers. Only by chance, when his father quarrelled with James Lamert, was he taken away. His mother, however, managed to smooth things over so that he might return: Charles never forgave her. 'My father said I should go back no more, and should go to school. I do not write resentfully or angrily: for I know how all these things have worked together to make me what I am: but I never afterwards forgot, I never shall forget, I never can forget, that my mother was warm for my being sent back.'[10] His parents must have felt guilt at their treatment of him, for they never spoke of the episode again. Nor, until he wrote his account of it to his friend and future biographer John Forster in 1847, did Dickens. 'I have never . . . in any burst of confidence with any one, my own wife not excepted, raised the curtain I then dropped, thank God.'[11]

The blacking factory left him with a lifelong insatiable need for recognition and approval; a degree of emotional reserve; and an obsession with cleanliness and order which he himself admitted was 'almost a *dis*order'.[12] He was haunted by the experience for the rest of his life. 'Even now, famous and caressed and happy, I often forget in my dreams that I have a dear wife and children; even that I am a man; and wander desolately back to that time of my life.'[13] The Christmas before his death, playing a 'memory game' with his family, Dickens wrote down, without explanation, 'Warren's Blacking, 30, Strand', which meant nothing to his children until his biography was published after his death.

The family's affairs did not improve, and the familiar round of changed lodgings, debts and difficulties continued. Fanny's fees at the Academy were not paid, and she had to leave for a while, returning to earn her singing tuition by giving piano lessons. But Charles was, as his father had promised, sent to school.

Wellington House Academy in the Hampstead Road was not a good school. The headmaster, Mr Jones, was an ignorant and violent man who beat the boys and bullied the staff, and Dickens drew on his memories when writing *David Copperfield*, where the school becomes Salem House. But it was a school of sorts, and he was determined to enjoy it. His contemporaries remembered him as a cheerful boy, agreeable and friendly, but not particularly studious, involved in jokes and games and amateur theatricals. Clearly, he was applying himself to the study of being a boy; but probably, like many clever students, he worked harder at his books than his friends realized. He spent two-and-a-half years there, leaving soon after his fifteenth birthday to begin the world in earnest.

Dickens's first job, as a solicitor's clerk, provided experiences which proved useful for his fiction, from *Pickwick Papers* onwards; but he had no intention of remaining there. He was educating himself in ways which had nothing to do with the law. He often walked the streets late into the night, a habit which he continued for many years. His friends were astonished at the extent to which he was already familiar with the street life of London, not knowing that his wanderings had begun in the desperate loneliness of his neglected childhood. Now he began to turn his acute eye and ear to good account, listening to the conversations and noting the appearance of ordinary Londoners.

He also expanded his more conventional self-education. A reader's ticket for the British Museum Library opened a wide field of literature and history. He also taught himself shorthand. Before he was seventeen he had left clerking and moved on to become a freelance shorthand reporter at the law courts of Doctors' Commons, where he saw at close quarters the law's interminable delays, later satirized in *Bleak House*. With this experience, he was equipped to find posts as a reporter of parliamentary debates.

Dickens originally owed his journalistic appointments to a series of fortunate introductions. His uncle, John Barrow, was the founder and editor of the *Mirror of Parliament*, one of the papers for which he worked; a lifelong friend, Thomas Beard, worked for the *Morning Chronicle*. But he had an excellent memory and a determination to succeed, and soon made a reputation for himself as a rapid and accurate reporter. His time in the press gallery of the House of Commons, from 1831 to 1834, gave him an invaluable education in politics. It also reinforced his interest in social reform, as he listened to the 1833 debates on the Factory Act, limiting hours of work, and the Poor Law Amendment Act, which set up the workhouse system he attacked in *Oliver Twist*. Though his early campaigning fiction and journalism did aim to change various aspects of statutory law, he was not impressed by the parliamentary process.

Dickens was never simply an industrious apprentice: he also enjoyed all the pleasures of London. He went to music-halls; he relished parties and dances. Though he was, in later life, a moderate, even abstemious drinker, he recorded vivid memories of getting drunk for the first time. He was still stage-struck, and he haunted the London theatres. He was especially impressed by the comedian Charles Mathews, who gave one-man shows in which he played contrasting characters, brought to life by subtle variations of gesture, accent and turn of phrase; he used such memories when he came to give the famous 'readings' of his last years. Sometimes Dickens would himself take parts at a private theatre where amateurs could act on payment of a fee.

In the summer of 1832 he nearly became a professional actor, when he applied for an audition at Covent Garden Theatre. Providentially he missed his appointment because of a bad cold. He might well have been successful, for he was a first-rate mimic, and his acting ability and stage presence were equal to that of many professionals of the day. An old stage carpenter, watching him give one of his electrifying amateur performances, once remarked, 'Ah, Mr Dickens, it was a sad loss to the public when you took to writing.'[14]

At the age of eighteen Dickens met the girl with whom he was seriously in love for over three years. Maria Beadnell, a banker's daughter, at first returned his feelings, and they became unofficially engaged. Dickens later gave an account of the affair, much of it conducted clandestinely through a friend of Maria's, in David's wooing of Dora in *David Copperfield*. Maria's parents were not impressed with the impecunious young man: no doubt they had discovered his father's lamentable financial record. Maria's feelings cooled, and Dickens, deeply hurt by her heartlessness, broke off the engagement soon after his twenty-first birthday.

He did not recover easily. His two early experiences of rejection left a deep, unhealed emotional fissure which was to have far-reaching effects on his life. But the Beadnells' judgement of him had also fuelled his ambition. He was soon to prove them wrong.

T W O

THE MAKING
OF 'BOZ',
1 8 3 2 – 4 0

Dickens's professional writing career began shortly before his twenty-second birthday, when a comic fictional sketch was accepted by the *Monthly Magazine*. Twelve years later he recalled seeing his work in print for the first time: 'my eyes were so dimmed with joy and pride, that they could not bear the street, and were not fit to be seen there'.[1] Six more sketches followed. When, in August 1834, he moved to his job on the *Morning Chronicle*, the editor encouraged him to write further 'street sketches' in addition to his political and news reporting. For these, Dickens started to use the pseudonym 'Boz'.

A salary of 5 guineas a week, with extra payment for his sketches, should have made Dickens financially secure: he considered the same amount a handsome salary to offer Wilkie Collins in 1856. But in November 1834 his father was once again arrested for debt. This time, the young man took matters into his own hands. He scraped together enough money to pay his father's debts and care for his mother (characteristically, John Dickens disappeared without trace for a while, prompting fears of his suicide). Then he finally separated himself, moving out of the fifteenth address the family had lived in since his birth into rooms in Furnival's Inn.

He was thus by the age of twenty-three fully independent, conscious that he could depend on no one but himself, but with a good appreciation of his own abilities. He appeared to have overcome his earlier physical frailty. Thanks to his love of walking he had a healthy outdoor complexion and carried himself well. He was becoming something of a dandy, always carefully dressed and meticulously clean. He sported a blue cloak with velvet facings, and became known for the bright colours of his fancy waistcoats. His brown hair fell about his face in fashionable ringlets. It is not surprising that he made an impression on the young daughters of George Hogarth, the editor of the *Evening Chronicle*, when he met them in the winter of 1834.

George Hogarth appreciated Dickens as a rising young author, and predicted his future success. His daughters were all entranced by the young man's energetic and entertaining personality. For him, the Hogarths were a substitute for his own unsatisfactory family. When he proposed to Catherine, the eldest daughter and the only one of marriageable age, he was in a sense proposing himself as a member of her family, as well as a husband. He was at once accepted.

Catherine was a plump, pretty girl, sweet-natured and rather passive. Her little sister Georgina, only seven years old, was already the live wire of the family. Dickens had energy enough for two, and there is no doubt that they were genuinely in love. Yet he was not, this time, infatuated; from the beginning the relationship was always on his terms. His work would come before everything else, something Catherine often found hard to accept. Dickens was in no hurry to be married, and they were engaged for almost a year. Catherine was only nineteen, and Dickens was cautious. He had suffered the effects of an improvident marriage, and had no intention of repeating his parents' mistakes.

Dickens's first published book was a collection of his newspaper sketches of London life and characters. *Sketches by Boz* was published on 8 February 1836, the day after his twenty-fourth birthday, with illustrations by George Cruikshank, a well-established and popular cartoonist and illustrator. The book was an immediate success. Two days later a representative of the publishers Chapman & Hall called on Dickens, and asked him to write some text to accompany a series of drawings by another comic artist, Robert Seymour, to be published in shilling monthly numbers. Dickens boldly insisted that the text must take priority, and that he must have the freedom to develop his ideas as he chose. So evolved *The Pickwick Papers*, the book which made his name.

Publication in monthly numbers, at that time rather scorned by serious writers, became thereafter Dickens's favourite form of publication. His success induced other novelists, Thackeray among them, to use it. With a rough outline of the plot and characters sketched in advance, it gave him the flexibility to change direction when necessary, responding to his readers' reactions, always keeping an eye on the sales figures.

Two days after the first number of *Pickwick* appeared on 31 March 1836, Dickens and Catherine Hogarth were married. The date was chosen by Dickens to fit in with his *Pickwick* schedule. After a week's honeymoon in a cottage near Rochester they began married life in Furnival's Inn, in a slightly larger set of chambers than his old ones.

The sales of *Pickwick Papers* were disappointing at first. The project might have foundered altogether when Robert Seymour committed suicide with only two numbers completed. However, Chapman & Hall had enough faith in Dickens to find another illustrator, Charles Hablôt Browne, who took the pseudonym 'Phiz' to match Dickens's 'Boz'. It proved the start of a long and happy association. The fortunes of *Pickwick Papers* and Dickens's future as a popular writer were assured with the sixth monthly number, when Dickens invented the character of Sam Weller. Perhaps borrowing the name of his story-telling nurse for Mr Pickwick's idiosyncratic cockney servant, he created one of the great comic characters of English literature, a nineteenth-century Sancho Panza. It was largely Weller, with his characteristic 'Wellerisms', who carried the readers with him through the loosely connected episodes.

Pickwick Papers was modelled on the picaresque novels of Smollett that Dickens had read as a child, and conveys an unforgettably lively picture of pre-Victorian England, about to be swept away by the railway era. At the same time its good-humoured atmosphere, softening the brutal comedy of the eighteenth century, links it with the gentler manners of the Victorian middle class. It was a winning formula.

The final number of *Pickwick Papers* for November 1837 sold 40,000 copies. Chapman & Hall brought out the book edition in the same month. They gave a 'Pickwick' dinner for the young author – the first of the many banquets held in his honour – and paid Dickens more than £2,000 above the sum they had initially agreed. To his delight, his old Chatham schoolmaster, William Giles, sent him a snuff-box inscribed to 'The Inimitable Boz', a phrase he immediately adopted as his favourite description of himself.

With his usual energy Dickens had meanwhile

written the libretto of an opera and the text of a farce, both given successful professional productions during 1836. He had also begun to edit a new magazine, *Bentley's Miscellany*, for the publisher Richard Bentley, providing instalments of his new novel, *Oliver Twist*, for the magazine while still writing *Pickwick*. In January 1837 Catherine gave birth to their first child, Charles Dickens junior. Their life seemed set on a prosperous and happy course, and they moved from the modest rooms in Furnival's Inn to 48 Doughty Street (now the Dickens Museum) in April 1837. A month later they were struck by a wholly unexpected tragedy.

Mary Hogarth, Catherine's seventeen-year-old sister, who often stayed with the young couple in the first year of their marriage, came to live with them when they moved to Doughty Street. In May, after a visit to the theatre, to see Dickens's farce *Is She His Wife?,* Mary became suddenly ill. She died in a few hours, in Dickens's arms. He was so devastated by her death that he was unable to work for a while, and the June instalments of *Pickwick Papers* and *Oliver Twist* had to be postponed. He took a ring off Mary's finger and wore it on his own hand, kept all her clothes, and hoped to be buried in her grave. For months he dreamed of her every night. The dreams ended abruptly when he told Catherine about them in a letter.

Such intensity of feeling might suggest that Dickens was in love with Mary and already dissatisfied with his marriage. His emotions were in fact more complicated. He seems to have cherished an ideal of sexless love for a sister-figure who would devote herself selflessly to him, a fantasy bound up with the lost Eden of the Chatham years and his relationship with his sister Fanny. Even as an adult, this pure love was something he yearned for, in a Wordsworthian association of childhood and true intensity of emotion. Catherine, a wife and mother, could no longer fulfil this dream. Real mothers were for him inevitably flawed; doomed to become the betrayers of innocence. Mary, for whose gravestone he wrote the description 'Young, Beautiful and Good', became the inspiration for the idealized innocent girls in his novels who are never shown as mature married women, most notably the tragic figure of Little Nell in *The Old Curiosity Shop*. Mary's death had its first effect on his writing in *Oliver Twist*, with the character of Rose Maylie, who almost dies of a severe illness but survives, apparently because of the intensity of Oliver's – and the author's – need for her to live.

Oliver Twist was Dickens's first fully crafted novel. Mounting a direct attack on the impersonal cruelty of the workhouse system, Dickens contrasts it with an ideal of individual benevolence. He also used the novel to reflect on his own early life. Taking the emotional rather than the literal truth of his experiences, he imagined what might have happened to a child set adrift in London, friendless and penniless. He had not become a criminal, and neither does Oliver; but Dickens emphasizes the attractions as well as the dangers of the underworld for such a child. Oliver, who has been starved of food and love since his birth, punished for asking for more, meets for the first time with warmth, good food, companionship and apparent affection in Fagin's thieves' kitchen. Even the pickpockets' practice sessions seem an enjoyable children's game. The disillusionment is all the more intense when Oliver discovers the cynical reality.

Dickens grafted realistic portraits of low life on to a theme of fairy-story simplicity: that of the child lost and found again. To emphasize his points he drew on the theatrical traditions of the melodramas he had seen in Chatham and London; the magazine instalments became the equivalent of stage scenes in which good and evil are starkly opposed. The novel sold well, and increased his popularity, though some reviewers thought his portraits of low-life characters debasing. In particular he was attacked for showing, in the relationship between Nancy and Bill Sikes, that a prostitute could feel a love for a thug and murderer that was as deep as any emotion experienced by her more respectable sisters.

Perennially anxious about money, and with a growing family (his second child, Mary, known as Mamie, was born on 6 March 1838), Dickens was now taking on an impossible variety of commitments. He had promised novels to three publishers at once, and this conflict of interests soon landed him in trouble. The intricacies of the subsequent negotiations are too complicated to give here, but the upshot was that Dickens quarrelled violently with Richard Bentley, the first of many disagreements with his publishers. He was already irritated by Bentley's interference with his editorship of *Bentley's Miscellany*, and he resigned from the magazine in January 1839.

It was at this time that his close friend and constant companion the journalist John Forster began to be invaluable to Dickens as an unofficial business manager and agent, helping to sort out his affairs. It took time to disentangle himself completely from Bentley, who continued to advertise a novel, *Barnaby Rudge*, on which Dickens had suspended work, though his next novel, *Nicholas Nickleby*, was published by Chapman & Hall.

Dickens's money worries had substance. He was still being plagued by his father, who embarrassed him by approaching his friends for money. 'How long he is growing up to be a man!' he complained.[2] His brother Frederick was equally feckless. When Dickens discovered that his father had approached Chapman & Hall for a loan, he exploded. He decided the only solution was to rusticate his parents, as far from London as practicable. Deciding on Devon, he installed them in a cottage near Exeter, providing them with an adequate, but not generous allowance. It proved only a temporary respite.

Oliver Twist was not completed until November 1839, but Dickens had already begun another, entirely different novel, *Nicholas Nickleby*, which began to appear in April 1838. His fiction was by now so popular that the first monthly number sold 50,000 copies. The novel contains a higher proportion of comedy to melodrama than *Oliver Twist*, and Dickens worked off some of his irritation with his parents by using aspects of his mother – her inappropriately youthful dress and inconsequential manner – for the character of the talkative and slightly senile Mrs Nickleby. Many of those who knew her thought he had been unfair. Elizabeth Dickens herself was happily unaware of the caricature, refusing to believe that such a woman could ever have existed. The main thrust of the novel, however, was Dickens's attack on the Yorkshire boarding schools. These schools, run by unscrupulous entrepreneurs, had sprung up to cater for children, often illegitimate, whose parents wanted to dispose of them cheaply.

It was Dickens's most successful single-handed campaign. The horrific regime at Dotheboys Hall may seem exaggerated, but was based on Bowes Academy, which Dickens himself visited on a fact-finding tour with his illustrator, Hablôt Browne. Though the proprietor William Shaw had been prosecuted in 1832 for his treatment of his pupils, the school had continued to exist. After the publication of *Nicholas Nickleby* it was forced to close, as were most of the similar Yorkshire schools.

A second daughter, Kate, was born to Charles and Catherine in October 1839, six days after the volume publication of *Nicholas Nickleby*. At the end of the year they moved from the house in Doughty Street to 1 Devonshire Terrace, Regent's Park, their home for the next eleven years. Here Dickens had a comfortable book-lined study, with a door leading into the garden where he played games of cricket and battledore and shuttlecock with his children. It was a house for a family, and for a man whose place in the world was assured.

Dickens was now firmly established in society, even if he was not quite *of* it. Entertained by fashionable London eager to bag the new literary lion, he and Catherine began to reciprocate with formal dinner parties at Devonshire Terrace. Jane Carlyle thought these rather too grand: 'such getting up of the steam is unbecoming to a literary man.'[3] Others found Dickens's fondness for jewelry, his flamboyant waistcoats and his carefully combed long hair slightly vulgar. In 1843 Thackeray saw him at a ball and reported 'how splendid Mrs Dickens was in pink satin & Mr Dickens in geranium and ringlets'.[4]

But there were many sides to Dickens. In an informal setting he was wonderful company, though the fun could turn unsettlingly manic. On a family holiday at Broadstairs he terrorized a young woman by holding her, struggling, at the edge of the sea as the tide rose to her knees, ruining her only silk dress. The same woman noticed the variability of his moods. 'His eyes were always like "danger lamps",' she remembered.[5]

Organizing family amateur dramatics, and at children's parties, he was at his best. He performed miraculous conjuring tricks and induced the most unlikely adults – Thackeray and Jane Carlyle among them – to waltz and polka until they dropped. His children adored him at such times; yet in private his mania for order was oppressive. He carried out daily inspections of children's hands, clothes and rooms, going through drawers and cupboards. The children came to dread the 'pincushion notes' left if he found any untidiness in their bedrooms.

External order was a thin crust over boiling imaginative chaos. In Dickens's next novel, *The Old Curiosity Shop*, almost all the characters who surround

Little Nell are grotesques from the world of nightmare. Even her own grandfather turns from a loving friend to a sinister enemy when he steals her painfully earned money. *The Old Curiosity Shop* is often criticized for sentimentality, but it is closer to the fairy-tales of Grimm than to those of Hans Andersen.

The death of Nell was foreshadowed through several episodes. 'I am slowly murdering that poor child', Dickens wrote.[6] In a period when many children died, it provoked tremendous emotion throughout England. Among Dickens's friends, the distinguished judge Lord Jeffrey wept unrestrainedly and the actor William Macready, who had recently lost his own daughter, found it hard to forgive Dickens for Nell's fate. Dickens himself said he was, 'breaking his heart over this story'.[7] But, though it brought Mary Hogarth's death vividly before him, he evoked this emotion deliberately. He knew his distress was intimately related to his creativity. '[I]t has borne a terrible, frightful, horrible proportion to the quickness of the gifts you remind me of. But may I not be forgiven for thinking it a wonderful testimony to my being made for my art, that when, in the middle of this trouble and pain, I sit down to my book, some beneficent power shows it all to me, and tempts me to be interested, and I don't invent it – really do not – *but see it*, and write it down.'⁸

The Old Curiosity Shop was originally planned as a short story for a new fiction magazine, *Master Humphrey's Clock*, which Dickens intended to adapt from the eighteenth-century model of the *Tatler* or *Spectator*, with the individual stories connected by the personality of a fictional narrator. The old-fashioned formula was not popular, and Dickens could not find suitable contributors. In the event, he wrote the entire magazine himself. Apart from some now forgotten stories, including an attempt to revive *Pickwick*, it consisted of *The Old Curiosity Shop* and the long-postponed *Barnaby Rudge*.

He found it difficult to switch to a new project after the emotional strain of *The Old Curiosity Shop*, and progress on *Barnaby Rudge* was slow. The burden of weekly production was exhausting, and he was not well. John Dickens's Devon exile ended without curing his incorrigible irresponsibility, and the money troubles rumbled on over the years. It was as much the unpredictable and uncontrollable element as the financial one that Dickens could not bear. Just when things were going well, his father would pop up, like Quilp, to plague him once more. 'Nothing makes me so wretched . . . as these things,' Dickens confessed. 'They are so entirely beyond my control, so far out of my reach, such a drag-chain on my life . . . He, and all of them, look upon me as something to be plucked and torn to pieces for their advantage.'[9] For the rest of his life John Dickens continued to run up debts, approach Dickens's friends for loans, and protest, to anyone who would listen, how badly his son treated him.

In October Dickens endured, without anaesthetic, a painful operation for a fistula, which interrupted the writing of *Barnaby Rudge*. With his usual determination he recovered in three weeks, finished the novel, and soon completed the plans for his next venture, a tour of North America. There was a growing appetite for travel books about the USA, and Chapman & Hall agreed that a book by Dickens describing the country, its inhabitants, and their institutions would be popular. Dickens was determined to be more positive than earlier, critical English visitors. Ironically, he was to be seen as the most unfair and negative of them all.

AMERICA
AND ITALY,
1842–6

Dickens and Catherine left for America in January 1842, and were away for six months, leaving their four children in lodgings in the charge of a governess and Dickens's younger brother Frederick. The baby, Walter, was still less than a year old. Their days were spent with the Macreadys' large family. It was not a happy arrangement, for the Macreadys were unusually strict parents. The Dickens children were consoled by frequent visits from their fifteen-year-old aunt, Georgina Hogarth, and became so fond of her that from the autumn of

1843 she became a permanent part of the Dickens household.

Dickens arrived in Boston to a welcome unprecedented in that staid city. 'There never was, and never will be, such a triumph,'[1] he was told. He and Catherine were overwhelmed with invitations and had to shake hands with hundreds of people every day. Crowds lined the streets to see him and cheered when he went to the theatre. Deputations came to see him from 2,000 miles away. He was besieged by ladies begging locks of his hair, and hardly dared have it cut, in case the barber sold the sweepings. After a month he found this 'Boz mania' and the consequent restrictions on his freedom intolerable, and decided to accept no more public engagements. He did, however, meet most of the important literary figures of the day, including Longfellow and Washington Irving, and had two long interviews with Edgar Allan Poe. He visited schools, orphanages, asylums and penal institutions, as well as factories, many of which compared favourably with those in England. He travelled extensively by train and riverboat, not much enjoying either, as far west as St Louis, south to Richmond, and ending in Canada, where both he and

Catherine took part in amateur theatricals at Montreal. Dickens, who took charge of the production, was surprised and delighted with her success as an actress.

Dickens was initially charmed by the cleanliness of Boston, the intellectual refinement of its inhabitants, and the humanity of its institutions. The conservative New England worthies did not return the compliment, privately finding in his gusto for life 'a considerable touch of rowdyism'.[2] They were glad to hand him on to the less refined citizens of New York. Dickens's own early enthusiasm turned to criticism as he saw more of America. Though he found the American people individually generous, hospitable and kind, he loathed the insanitary habit of spitting, then almost universal, and disliked the over-heated homes and public buildings. When he visited the Philadelphia Eastern Penitentiary, he was appalled at the system which kept prisoners in solitude, without work or distraction of any kind, for the whole of their sentences. He believed the authorities did not understand the psychological effects. '[T]here is a depth of terrible endurance in it . . . which no man has a right to inflict upon his fellow-creature. I hold this slow and daily tampering with the mysteries of the brain, to be immeasurably worse than any torture of the body: and because its ghastly signs and tokens are not so palpable to the eyes and sense of touch as scars upon the flesh . . . therefore I the more denounce it, as a secret punishment which slumbering humanity is not roused up to stay.'[3] He was also, like most English visitors, shocked by slavery. The manifest inequality of the slaves seemed to him to make the Declaration of Independence a 'monstrous lie'.[4]

Dickens found Americans complacent about the lack of copyright protection for foreign authors. When he expressed his opinions he caused such outrage that he came to believe there was less freedom of speech in the USA than in any other civilized country. In spite of its virtues, the country disappointed his radical hopes. 'The Nation is a body without a head and the arms and legs are occupied in quarrelling with the trunk and each other.'[5] His hosts felt that after his hero's welcome, it was ill-mannered of Dickens to take them to task in public. His willingness to speak out against abuses in England, part of the reason for his popularity in the USA, was not so welcome on their home ground.

Dickens and Catherine returned to England in June and were joyfully reunited with their children. Their eldest son Charley, now five years old, was so overcome at seeing his parents that he fell into convulsions, and the doctor was called. Fortunately he quickly recovered, and the family, soon augmented by Georgina Hogarth, settled into a domestic routine, while Dickens began his travel book, *American Notes*.

Though Dickens was often forced by pressure of work to write all day, and sometimes late into the night, he preferred to write in the mornings, think about his work while walking energetically in the afternoons, and relax in the evenings. He took frequent holidays with his family, often at Broadstairs, his favourite seaside town. He also travelled round Britain with friends such as John Forster and Daniel Maclise. But holidays never interrupted his writing. Arriving in a new place he immediately organized his working environment, laying out pens, paper and blue ink in his regular pattern.

Dickens thought *Martin Chuzzlewit*, the novel he began that winter, by far the best he had written, but sales were disappointing. Even the last-minute decision to send his hero to America failed to improve them greatly, though the savagely satirical episodes describing Martin's doomed attempts to make his fortune in the swamps of Louisiana made him laugh aloud as he wrote. The characters of the nurse Mrs Gamp and the hypocritical Mr Pecksniff have become a part of literary legend, but *Martin Chuzzlewit* is a dark and uneven novel, betraying signs of exhaustion. Though reviews were generally favourable, a trade depression in 1843, and Chapman & Hall's failure to advertise the novel as widely as his earlier works, probably affected volume sales. There was a predictably hostile reaction in the USA.

Dickens's feeling for his public's taste was, however, vindicated by the universal success of *A Christmas Carol*, the first of his 'Christmas Books', published in December 1843. Though his own appetite for food and drink was far from gargantuan, it was in this story he invented, almost single-handedly, the myth of 'the English Christmas', overflowing with good things: a season of universal reconciliation. The allegory of the redemption of the misanthropist Scrooge, and his conversion to the spirit of Christmas is a simple, even childish idea. Only Dickens would have shown the origins of Scrooge's hard-heartedness in his own sufferings as a neglected and unloved child.

The emphasis in *A Christmas Carol* was once more on private philanthropy as an antidote to the cold impersonality of state institutions. Dickens practised what he preached. Though he continued to advocate public action on social affairs, writing a letter to the *Morning Chronicle* arguing vehemently for an Act of Parliament to regulate the employment of women and children in mines, he also made numerous speeches at charity dinners and undertook private benefactions. To give only one example of many: his efforts raised over £2,000 for the orphaned children of an actor, Edward Elton. He was also roused to indignant action by a visit to the 'Ragged Schools' set up to offer basic literacy to the poorest of the poor. The teachers, who funded the pathetically inadequate schools out of their own pockets, did their best, but Dickens was horrified by 'the dire neglect of soul and body exhibited in these children . . . To find anything within them – who know nothing of affection, care, love, or kindness of any sort – to which it is possible to appeal, is, at first, like a search for the philosopher's stone.'[6]

He was convinced that the usual church charities were useless. These children needed to be fed and clothed, taught basic concepts of right and wrong, not made to parrot the catechism. England's neglect of universal primary education was not only wicked, but dangerous. 'I lose belief in the possibility of the progress, or even of the long existence, of an Empire, with such a mighty crime and danger at its heart.'[7] The ragged boy and girl, Ignorance and Want, in *A Christmas Carol* were not exaggerated; he had seen them, and worse.

Dickens continued to visit the 'Ragged Schools' and campaign on their behalf, enlisting the heiress Angela Burdett-Courts in his fight to support them. Miss Coutts, two years his junior, had met Dickens in 1835, and was godmother to his eldest son. She inherited her grandfather's immense fortune, with an income of over £50,000 a year; a sum unimaginable in today's values. She used her money well, becoming the greatest philanthropist of the age. For many years Dickens acted as her confidential agent in her charitable enterprises, sorting the thousands of begging-letters into the genuine and the dubious, and directing her attention to worthy individuals and causes.

By the close of 1843 Dickens had determined to move his whole family to Italy for a year, even though his fifth child, Francis, made a not very welcome appearance in January 1844. Forster, fearing he would lose his public, was against it. Dickens argued that he wanted to live privately for a while, and his living expenses would be half what they were in London. Working at the rate he had done for the past eight years, he explained, 'leaves a horrible despondency behind, when it is done'.[8] He made the risky decision not to write another full-length novel for two years.

Dickens was now dissatisfied with his latest publishers, Chapman & Hall. *A Christmas Carol*, though immensely popular, had not earned him as much as he had expected. He therefore transferred to the firm of Bradbury & Evans, the publishers of *Punch*, who were prepared to advance him £2,800, for which his only obligation was to write another Christmas Book. The house in Devonshire Terrace was let for the year, and at the beginning of July 1844 Dickens and Catherine, the five children, Georgina Hogarth, a courier, and three servants travelled by leisurely stages to Genoa. Though he returned to

England from time to time, Dickens was to be more abroad than at home until the spring of 1847.

Dickens relaxed as energetically as he did everything else, squeezing every ounce of interest and pleasure out of the Italian adventure. The family were settled at the Palazzo Peschiere in Genoa, a splendid, if rather faded, mansion. Dickens and Catherine took Italian lessons, though he deliberately avoided contact with Italian society, and he began work on his Christmas Book, *The Chimes*. He intended it to be 'a great blow for the Poor'[9] and its satiric attack on the obtuse self-satisfaction of the comfortable classes caused considerable controversy. Dickens was accused of stirring up class hatred and encouraging mob violence; he was also praised for his hard-hitting attack.

As soon as his work was done, Dickens, incorrigibly restless, was off. Leaving his family behind, he first travelled alone through Italy. Like most travellers he was entranced by his first sight of Venice. But he was soon homesick for England, explaining to Forster: 'that unspeakable restless something . . . would render it almost as impossible for me to remain here . . . as it would be for a full balloon, left to itself, not to go up.'[10] He made a brief visit to London, during which he read *The Chimes* to a gathering of friends on two occasions, with great success. This, with his acting triumph at Montreal, reawakened his ambitions as a performer. By 1846 he was already thinking of giving public readings from his own books.

In the spring of 1845 Dickens and Catherine made a tour of Italy, Georgina joining them for part of the journey. The three of them made a terrifying ascent of Vesuvius while it was erupting, Dickens going right to the rim of the exploding crater, Catherine and Georgina having their clothes torn to rags on the descent. But the most unusual adventure of Dickens's year in Italy was his hypnotic treatment of Madame de la Rue, the English wife of a Swiss banker living in Genoa.

Augusta de la Rue suffered from hysterical tics and convulsions which would have intrigued Freud. Dickens, who had already discovered that he was able to hypnotize Catherine, now tried his powers on his friend. He found he could 'magnetize' her – put her into a hypnotic trance – and relieve her sufferings by getting her to describe what she felt and saw in this condition. She felt herself pursued by a bad phantom, which was somehow confused with memories of her brother. Dickens was already fascinated by the power of past experiences on human nature, and seems to have conducted a primitive, rather dangerous, form of psychoanalysis which did have a temporary effect on Madame de la Rue's symptoms, though they later returned by degrees and became as severe as before. He even claimed to be able to 'magnetize' her at a distance. The episode had a deep significance for him, which was more to do with his own psychology than with that of Madame de la Rue. Someone who knew both women thought Madame de la Rue resembled Dickens's sister Fanny.

Though Catherine had always been sensible enough not to take seriously his penchant for over-dramatic comic flirtations, she was disturbed by his relationship with Augusta de la Rue, and objected to the intensity of it. Dickens reacted angrily: it caused the first serious rift between them. Nine years later Dickens was still resentful. He insisted that 'the intense pursuit of any idea that takes complete possession of me, is one of the qualities that makes me different . . . from other men. Whatever made you unhappy in the Genoa time had no other root, beginning, middle, or end, than whatever has made you proud and honored in your married life.'[11]

The Dickens family returned to England in the summer of 1845. Catherine was once more pregnant. Dickens was full of ideas for an amateur dramatic society in which his friends and relations would be the actors, with himself as actor-manager. By August rehearsals of Ben Jonson's *Every Man in his Humour*, with Dickens in the key role of the boastful Bobadil, were under way. Though Dickens fretted at the badness of his fellow-actors, the single performance at the Royalty Theatre on 20 September was a great success. *The Times* got wind of the private production, and reviewed it favourably, particularly praising Dickens's performance. The excitement and immediacy of public performance was addictive: it soon became a regular part of his life.

As regular additions to the family continued to appear, Dickens regarded them as increasingly unwelcome visitations of fate. Catherine's sixth child, Alfred, was born in October 1845. The seventh, Sydney, arrived in April 1847. This was a particularly difficult birth, and the Queen's *accoucheur* was called in. Eight months later, Catherine miscarried in the train between Glasgow and Edinburgh, where Dickens addressed a large meeting. Dickens sought the advice of the famous surgeon Sir James Simpson, the pioneer of anaesthesia, and learned from him of the successful use of chloroform in childbirth. He was more interested, however, in his Edinburgh success than in Catherine's illness. 'The inimitable did wonders,' he wrote while she was still convalescent. 'I have . . . never enjoyed myself more completely.'[12]

Just over a year later another son, Henry, was born. Again, the baby 'did not come into the world as he ought to have done'.[13] At Dickens's insistence, and against the advice of the London doctors, Catherine was successfully given chloroform. A daughter, Dora, was born in 1850, and a tenth and final child, Edward, nicknamed 'Plorn', in 1852. With a total of ten babies and at least two miscarriages in sixteen years, Catherine was all too frequently in an *un*interesting condition, as Dickens put it.

Hans Andersen, meeting Catherine in 1847, described her as 'a little stout' but 'with such an intensely good face that one at once felt confidence in her'.[14] Lord Jeffrey, who urged Dickens to have no more children, thought her 'true-hearted and affectionate'.[15] Most of their friends agreed. But, as pregnancy followed pregnancy, Catherine inevitably became less of a companion for her husband. Though he was still affectionate and concerned, he found her lethargy irritating, and turned for support and stimulus to Georgina. He saw in her some of the qualities of the earlier sister-figure, Mary Hogarth. 'So much of her spirit shines out in this sister', he told her mother, 'that the old time comes back again at some seasons, and I can hardly separate it from the present.'[16] But he was not in love with Georgina. She was to develop, rather, from 'my little pet' to 'my little housekeeper' to 'the best and truest friend man ever had'.[17] Georgina herself hero-worshipped Dickens. She never married, and dedicated her long life first to his service, and then to his memory.

The healthy Georgina, with her active intelligence and gift for wonderfully comic mimicry, was closer to a female version of Dickens himself than to his ideal of the fragile young girl, too good for this world. He found a better match to the pattern in Christiana Weller, a talented pianist. Dickens's conviction that she was destined for an early grave (she became the mother of two children, one the poet Alice Meynell, and lived to be eighty-five) was strengthened by her physical resemblance to Mary Hogarth. His feelings for Christiana during 1844 and 1845 were strong. But he was able to relinquish her without anguish, even urging her to marry. The fantasy came to an abrupt end when she was pregnant with her first child. Dickens complained: 'she is a mere spoiled child . . . Matrimony . . . certainly has not improved her.'[18] There were other, less serious, flirtations – Dickens was always extremely attractive to women and appreciative of them – but no suggestion of any real temptation to infidelity at this time.

In 1846 Dickens tried once more to fill an editor's chair, when Bradbury & Evans started the *Daily News*. He lasted three weeks. He could never row in anyone else's boat, and he was annoyed by Bradbury & Evans's interference. He did write some pieces on Italy for the paper, which became the basis for his travel book *Pictures from Italy*. He also contributed five important articles questioning capital punishment. He argued that the death penalty had a brutalizing effect, aroused morbid fascination, and led to sympathy with the criminal. He returned to the

Charles Dickens, by Samuel Laurence. (By courtesy of the National Portrait Gallery, London)

Charles Dickens's father, John Dickens. (Reproduced by courtesy of the Dickens House Museum, London)

Charles Dickens's mother, Elizabeth Dickens. (Reproduced by courtesy of the Dickens House Museum, London)

Catherine Dickens, at the time of her marriage. (Reproduced by courtesy of the Dickens House Museum, London)

Mary Hogarth, Charles Dickens's 'angel' sister-in-law. (Reproduced by courtesy of the Dickens House Museum, London)

'My little housekeeper', Georgina Hogarth, c. 1850, by Augustus Egg. (Reproduced by courtesy of the Dickens House Museum, London)

Charley, Mamie, Kate and Walter Dickens, 1842, by Daniel Maclise. (Reproduced by courtesy of the Dickens House Museum, London)

Dickens as the dying hero in *The Frozen Deep*. (Reproduced by courtesy of the Dickens
House Museum, London)

Dickens's last love, Nelly Ternan.
(V&A Picture Library)

Dickens giving a reading from his works. (Reproduced by courtesy of the Dickens House Museum, London)

Dickens with his daughters, in the garden at Gad's Hill Place. (Reproduced by courtesy of the Dickens House Museum, London)

Dickens in America, 1868. (Reproduced by courtesy of the Dickens House Museum, London)

theme in 1849, in letters to *The Times* describing the wickedness and levity of the crowd he witnessed at a public hanging. This time he was more cautious, calling only for the abolition of public hanging.

Freed from editorial commitments, he decided to go abroad once more, this time to Switzerland. The family settled near Lausanne, and Dickens embarked on *Dombey and Son*. The move was a mistake, for the quiet rural life dangerously depressed him. There was agreeable society at Lausanne, and he made new friends, but he missed the bustle of a big city: '*My* figures seem disposed to stagnate without crowds about them'.[19] He did not fully regain his spirits until November, when they moved to Paris for the winter. There, with visits to 'Hospitals, Prisons, Dead-houses, Operas, Theatres, Concert Rooms, Burial Grounds, Palaces and Wine Shops',[20] he rapidly recovered.

F O U R

THE CRITIC
OF SOCIETY,
1846–55

*D*ombey and Son appeared in monthly numbers
from September 1846 to March 1848, each
number selling over 30,000 copies. Comparisons
with Thackeray's *Vanity Fair*, also appearing in
numbers, were inevitable, but Thackeray himself
despaired of writing in competition with the power
of the early numbers of *Dombey*, and praised Dickens's
account of Dr Blimber's school, where little boys
were force-fed with knowledge: 'worth whole
volumes of Essays on the subject if Bigotry would
believe that laughs may tell truth'.[1]

The two-year break from producing novels had given Dickens the opportunity of writing in a more considered way. *Dombey and Son* was tightly structured. The main themes were worked out in advance, with the importance of the daughter who is 'better than any son at last'[2] emphasized. Dickens's attack was no longer aimed at specific social abuses, but at a climate of opinion that saw everything in terms of monetary value, viewing childhood as an irritating preliminary to the real 'business' of the world and marriage a matter of buying and selling. Throughout the novel the sea and the railways are used as insistent, perhaps over-emphatic, metaphors: the organic and eternal contrasted with the mechanical and inhuman.

When he returned with his family from the Continent in the spring of 1847 Dickens resumed his usual activities, and eagerly took up new enterprises. He became particularly closely involved with Miss Coutts's latest venture, a refuge to rehabilitate prostitutes, female ex-prisoners and women who were homeless and destitute. Similar homes had failed because they returned the women to the same environment. Dickens believed that emigration to the colonies, where women were badly needed, would be a better solution, and in *David Copperfield* Australia provides a happy ending for an improbably miscellaneous group of his characters. He was shocked to discover that candidates for the refuge were so ignorant that they did not understand the difference between transportation and emigration.

Dickens found a suitable house at Lime Grove, then semi-rural, which Miss Coutts renamed Urania Cottage. He intervened in the smallest details. It was he who interviewed prospective matrons; vetted the inmates for their suitability; insisted on gardens, a piano and singing-lessons; even chose the materials – in four cheerful colours – for the women's dresses. On religion he was not always in sympathy with Miss Coutts. He was convinced that scolding the women at Urania Cottage about their sinfulness would be counter-productive; he wanted them to look forward with hope to a happier future. He disliked much about the established church, particularly the High Church Puseyite wing, and for a number of years he deserted it altogether, attending a Unitarian chapel. Religion for Dickens was always a practical matter. 'The world is not a dream, but a reality, of which we are the chief part, and in which we must be up and doing something' and 'Our business is to use life well. If we do that we may leave Death alone',[3] he wrote in letters to a young woman who had morbid thoughts of death.

There were inevitable failures. Women fought, stole, absconded, lapsed into prostitution on the voyage to their new country. Nevertheless, in a *Household Words* article of 1853, Dickens claimed that of the fifty-six women who had passed through Urania Cottage in six years, thirty had successfully emigrated and done well.

Dickens's next novel, *David Copperfield*, his 'favourite child',[4] reflected his involvement in Urania Cottage with the 'fallen women' stories of Em'ly and Martha. It also related more closely to his own life than any of his other novels. During his year in Italy he had time to consider his life, and had begun to write some fragments of autobiography. In 1847, in response to a chance question from Forster, he revealed to him the shameful secret of the blacking warehouse. Over the following year they talked often about his childhood. Confiding in his friend encouraged Dickens to write more, and the slow death of his favourite sister Fanny from consumption in 1848 may have prompted further memories of their childhood. In his last Christmas book, *The Haunted Man*, published in December 1848, the hero is haunted by painful memories: an unloving childhood, betrayal by his best friend, the death of a loved sister. A ghostly likeness of himself offers him the chance to be freed from such memories, but he discovers that bad and good are inextricably bound up together. In forgetting past pain he ceases to be fully human. Worse, he has the same effect on those about him. Only a savage street-child, who has never become humanized by love, is unaffected. The allegory clearly had a relevance to Dickens's decision to explore the pain of his own childhood.

By 1849 he had organized his autobiographical fragments into a connected narrative, and thought about publishing it. He showed it to Catherine, who strongly urged him not to, because of his harsh criticism of his parents, especially his mother. Instead, the material was used in *David Copperfield*.

The relationship to Dickens's own experience in his most autobiographical novel was underlined by his decision to write it in the first person. The dual perspective of an older narrator looking back on his earlier self while keeping the sharp, fresh perceptions of the child and young man is managed with marvellous dexterity; with many of the early scenes written in the present tense, intimacy and distance are achieved simultaneously. He met Catherine's objections by recasting his parents as the Micawbers. Though he kept many of the events of their lives, and his father's actual words and habits of speech, neither the ludicrous but fundamentally benign Micawbers, nor David's charming but childish mother – the mother of Dickens's earliest memories – are responsible for his suffering, but the wholly fictional step-father and step-aunt Mr and Miss Murdstone.

Initially *David Copperfield* did not sell as well as *Dombey and Son*, but Dickens, who knew he was writing better than ever before, was not worried. He had a scheme to guarantee himself a secure income and a regular outlet for his social concerns. He had long been meditating a magazine, a popular weekly combining instruction with entertainment. This was now launched, with Bradbury & Evans as the publishers. Dickens himself was the editor, with W.H. Wills, a sound journalist from the staff of the *Daily*

News, as his assistant. Though Dickens was scornful of Wills's lack of imagination, he was a meticulous second-in-command who was invaluable in the day-to-day running of the magazine. Dickens had an income of £500 a year as editor, and a 50 per cent share in the paper. Wills and Forster had 25 per cent between them, leaving Bradbury & Evans with the remaining 25 per cent. Dickens was, for the first time, in complete control of a periodical.

By February 1850 the title *Household Words* had been decided, and Dickens was soliciting contributions from the leading writers and journalists of the day. All contributors were anonymous, and the magazine carried the running head 'Conducted by Charles Dickens' across the top of each page. Dickens 'conducted' the magazine in great detail, firmly imposing his own style. He painstakingly edited and rewrote his own work – he described his proofs as inky fishing-nets – and that of his contributors, taking particular trouble with young and inexperienced writers.

Household Words was the ideal vehicle to be pulled by his hobby-horses. His team of regular writers, with more occasional contributors, covered a wide range of interests. The magazine contained stories, poems, articles on art, literature, science and music, on modern inventions, aspects of history, matters of social interest or concern. Dickens himself contributed about a hundred articles and stories in the first two years. Dullness was the great sin. 'Brighten it, brighten it, brighten it!',[5] he exhorted Wills. In his first article he insisted that society must 'tenderly cherish that light of Fancy which is inherent in the human breast'.[6] His understanding of his public created one of the most successful magazines of the nineteenth century.

Once *David Copperfield* was finished, in October 1850, Dickens turned immediately to the agreeable business of amateur theatricals. This time the ostensible purpose was to raise funds for the newly conceived Guild of Literature and Art, which Dickens and the novelist Edward Bulwer-Lytton had devised as a way of providing pensions and sheltered housing for authors who had fallen on hard times. Houses were to be built at Knebworth, Lytton's Hertfordshire estate.

Bulwer-Lytton wrote a play, *Not so Bad as We Seem*, for the amateur company to perform; Dickens directed and played the lead. When W.H. Wills turned down the suggestion that he should play the small part of Dickens's valet, another of the actors, the painter Augustus Egg, suggested Wilkie Collins, just beginning to make his way as a writer.

Wilkie Collins was twelve years younger than Dickens. Unmarried, and at that time free from domestic commitments, he was very different in temperament from John Forster. Forster remained the loyal and discreet confidant on whom Dickens could always rely, but he was ponderous and censorious, convinced that he knew what was best for his friend. Forster could be loud and quarrelsome: mutual friends were sometimes shocked by the violence of his clashes with Dickens.

Collins was an easy-going companion, and his unconventional attitudes are reflected in the relaxed tone of Dickens's letters to him. With him Dickens could roam the streets of London and Paris, finding adventures and material for his writing in dubious music-halls and night spots. Collins was also an ardent disciple who wholeheartedly admired everything Dickens wrote. Dickens appreciated Collins's serious approach to writing, and he was soon co-opted as a regular contributor to *Household Words*, eventually becoming a staff writer. Later he was to collaborate with Dickens on articles, stories and plays. They became so successful at copying each other's writing styles that when Wilkie Collins was ill in 1862, Dickens offered to write the next number of his novel *No Name* for him.

The spring of 1851 brought Dickens a number of family anxieties. In March it became evident that Catherine was extremely unwell. She was suffering attacks of giddiness, with violent headaches, confusion and nervousness. Dickens sent her for spa treatment at Malvern. The regime, 'rigorous discipline of air, exercise, and cold water',[7] might have been devised by Dickens himself. In the same month John Dickens died after an agonizing operation, without anaesthetic, for a long-neglected stricture. Dickens, much more affected than he expected to be, behaved impeccably. He was present at his father's deathbed, promised his mother he would look after her, and settled John Dickens's debts for the last time – his assets were valued at less than £40.

In April, while Catherine was still at Malvern, their baby Dora, delicate since birth, had convulsions and died suddenly. The news was brought to Dickens, who had been playing with the child a few hours before, as he was making a speech at the annual dinner of the General Theatrical Fund. He wrote Catherine a carefully worded letter to prepare her for the news, and sent Forster to break it to her, while he sat all night beside his dead child. Comments in Dickens's letters on the irony of the deaths of the two Doras – first the child of his fancy in *David Copperfield*, then his real child – seem oddly detached, yet, though not as distraught as Catherine, he felt the loss of his daughter deeply.

The first night of *Not so Bad as We Seem* was postponed for a fortnight. The play was staged in May, in the presence of the Queen, at the London home of the Duke of Devonshire. Further London performances followed, and there was an extremely successful tour of the north of England the following year.

Dickens was also busy house-hunting, and in July he bought a lease of Tavistock House, Tavistock Square. He intended the business of moving house to be a distraction for Catherine, but he could not resist involving himself in the major renovations, making decisions on everything from structural alterations to the colour of the wallpapers. One essential in any house he occupied was a cold shower with an unlimited supply of water (Wilkie Collins later complained that the shower dripped all night and kept him awake). A new departure was a schoolroom, from the beginning designed as much for parties and amateur theatricals as for the education of his large family.

He began work on a new novel in September. *Bleak House*, the first of Dickens's satires on current British institutions, attacked the delays and obfuscations of the law, specifically the Court of Chancery, immediately evoked in the image of pervasive London fog which opens the novel. Making the bold attempt to write as a woman, he also highlighted the cruelty of stigmatizing illegitimacy, and returned to the scandal of destitute, ignorant street-children in the description of Jo the crossing-sweeper, who 'don't know nothink',[8] and pointing out the absurdity of sending missionaries to Africa while ignoring the children 'dying thus around us every day'.[9] *Bleak House* is also an early example of the detective novel, with Inspector Bucket as the first police detective in English fiction.

Bleak House sold better than any of Dickens's earlier novels, and for the next few years he was free from money worries. For the first time he moved his family to Boulogne for the summer of 1853. The Villa des Moulineaux was a charming, eccentric house, with several pavilions and summer-houses in the garden, which Dickens invited his friends to occupy. Among them were Wilkie Collins and Augustus Egg, a gentle, timid man, hopelessly in love with Georgina Hogarth. In October Dickens persuaded Egg and Collins to join him for a tour of France, Switzerland and Italy.

Dickens, the most experienced traveller of the three, was alternately amused and irritated by his companions, whose failings were detailed with relish in his letters home. Egg made vain attempts to master Italian. Collins, whose father was a well-known painter, made pretentious comments on art. They were disorganized, untidy and dirty; they complained of things for which there was no remedy, and were mean over trifling sums of money. Not sharing his restlessness, they would have preferred to stop and look about them, rather than always moving on. But it is clear that Dickens, as always the orchestrator of the journey, was also enjoying himself hugely, and the three mostly got on very well together.

Railways had not yet reached many parts of the Continent, and travel was still hazardous in Switzerland and parts of Italy. They travelled in a variety of extraordinary vehicles, 'like swings, like boats, like Noah's arks, like barges and enormous bedsteads'.[10] An excursion to Chamonix, with a precipice on each side of the track, the journey to Milan in an ancient carriage, when they each had to hold one end of a string attached to the luggage on top of the vehicle, for fear of thieves, and a voyage to Naples in a steamer so crowded that Egg and Collins had to sleep in the ship's stores – Dickens managed to bag the steward's cabin – were among the more unusual of their many adventures.

They returned to London in early December. At the end of the month Dickens gave three public readings of *A Christmas Carol* at Birmingham, in aid of the Literary and Scientific Institute. As soon as the new year began, he turned his attention once more to *Household Words*, for which he had written almost nothing during his long absence.

Without Dickens's contributions the circulation had dropped alarmingly. His remedy was a short novel, for weekly serialization. *Hard Times* worked the usual Dickens magic, and sales figures rose spectacularly with the first instalment. At first he was seized with enthusiasm for his subject, but soon confessed he found the difficulty of writing at that length 'CRUSHING. Nobody can have an idea of it who has not had an experience of patient fiction-writing with some elbow-room always.'[11]

Hard Times was dedicated to Thomas Carlyle, perhaps the most influential thinker on social affairs of the nineteenth century. Carlyle's attacks on Utilitarianism and 'the cash nexus' – the reduction of the relationship between employer and employee to a matter of money – are central to the novel, now one of Dickens's most popular. At the time it aroused mixed reactions. Macaulay condemned it as 'sullen socialism'[12] and Harriet Martineau considered Dickens did not have an adequate grasp of the issues, but Ruskin thought the novel should be studied by everyone interested in social problems. Acknowledging Dickens's habit of caricature and exaggeration, he went on, in a perceptive comment on Dickens's writing in general: 'let us not lose the use of Dickens's wit and insight because he chooses to write in a circle of stage fire. He is entirely right in his main drift and purpose in every book he has written'.[13]

Hard Times reflected Dickens's deepening despondency about the state of society. He was now totally disillusioned with the parliamentary process, and he refused many invitations to stand for Parliament, feeling he could be more effective through his writing. Though he was a founder-member of the Administrative Reform Association in 1855, he was also writing despairingly, 'representative government is become altogether a failure with us . . . English gentilities and subserviences render the people unfit for it'.[14] Education was the key: without that the people were not informed enough to make use of the ballot.

It became increasingly evident to his friends from 1854 onwards that in spite of his continuing popularity and success Dickens was dissatisfied with his personal life. Catherine irritated him more and more, and he was discovering that his children were not like the creations of his imagination. He could not design their characters, nor control their destinies. Dickens adored his children while they were babies, delighting in their directness, playing with them and giving them outlandish nicknames. But he confessed to 'a habit of suppression . . . which makes me chary of showing my affections, even to my children, except when they are very young'.[15] This emotional reserve especially affected his relationship with his sons, as he compared their advantages with his own early deprivation. The eldest, Charley, now seventeen, came home from learning German in Leipzig with no idea of what he wanted to do in life. 'I think he has less fixed purpose and energy than I could have supposed possible in my own son',[16] Dickens complained, suggesting his passivity was inherited from Catherine – though the same traits were evident in his own brothers. In the next decade his younger sons, with one exception, were to prove equally disappointing.

Dickens related better to his daughters. His favourite, Kate, who resembled her father closely in appearance, character and intelligence, was always permitted more licence than the other children, who often used her as a go-between with their father. Only Kate was not reprimanded when she was late for breakfast. Mamie, recovering from a serious illness, was allowed, very exceptionally, to be in his study while he was writing *Hard Times*. He was a restless and peripatetic writer: Mamie recalled watching him act out the character he was writing, making faces in the mirror and striding round the room muttering the dialogue.

Hard Times was finished in July 1854, on a family holiday at Boulogne. It left Dickens more dissatisfied than ever, with wild thoughts of getting away entirely by himself for six months. Only the usual release of walking fast and far saved him from exploding, he felt. He was to be unsettled further, in February 1855, by two incidents which forcibly recalled his early life.

THE END OF THE MARRIAGE, 1855–9

On 7 February 1855 Dickens celebrated his forty-third birthday with a dinner at Gravesend. Afterwards, as he walked through the snow to Rochester, he passed Gad's Hill Place, and saw it was for sale. Dickens had always remembered his father telling him, as a little boy at Chatham, that if he worked hard and became a great man, he might live in that grand country house one day. Now, though his father had not lived to see it, the dream could become reality.

Two days later, he had a letter from his first great love, Maria Beadnell. She was now married and a mother, but though she warned him that she was toothless, fat, old and ugly, he responded eagerly. They arranged to meet. This dream ended in disillusion, for Maria had told the truth. Worse, the middle-aged woman had kept the fluttering girlish manner that had once enchanted him and was now ludicrous. Dickens, dismayed, retreated rapidly, refusing her invitations and cutting short the correspondence. Rather cruelly he used Maria as the ridiculous Flora Finching, Arthur Clennam's early love, in his next novel, *Little Dorrit*.

Little Dorrit continued Dickens's attack on contemporary society. This time he was satirizing the deadening effect of bureaucracy on individual lives. As an ironic comment on the abdication of personal responsibility at all levels of society, he added the sub-title 'Nobody's Fault', and took a personal example from his own childhood, his father's financial irresponsibility and his imprisonment for debt, re-examining this more critically than in *David Copperfield*. His father was now dead, and Dickens's vision had become bleaker, his understanding of human nature more complex and less forgiving, since he had drawn the genial figure of Wilkins Micawber.

'The Father of the Marshalsea', the selfish, blinkered William Dorrit, who exploits his daughter Amy's cheerful self-sacrifice, shows the other side of John Dickens. Prisons, real and symbolic, haunt the novel, metaphors for the helplessness of the ordinary citizen, and an expression also of Dickens's increasing sense of entrapment in his marriage.

As usual, he found the early stages of writing the novel difficult, and turned in June to producing a melodrama, *The Lighthouse*, written by Wilkie Collins. The schoolroom at Tavistock House was used for the first time for a play performed by adults, to invited audiences. The scenery was designed by an old friend, the painter Clarkson Stanfield, and the actors were Dickens himself, his friends and his daughter Mamie, now aged seventeen. The production was a great success.

From the autumn of 1855 to the spring of 1856 Dickens moved his family to Paris, where Mamie and Kate were given the fashionable polish of Parisian society, and lessons from visiting French teachers. It was a continuation of their old-fashioned, ladylike upbringing. Though there were now good girls' schools in London, they were kept at home, with governesses and visiting tutors. Dickens's criticisms of the social order did not extend to the position of middle-class women. Though he respected working women, he pitied them; his daughters were not expected to earn a living, though Kate later had to do so, but to marry suitably and become ideal wives and mothers.

Their brothers were treated very differently. With his own brothers still making financial demands on him, Dickens was desperate that his sons should follow his example and stand on their own feet as soon as possible. After early lessons with Georgina, they were all sent away to schools in England and Boulogne. Even the youngest and dearest, Plorn, went to boarding school at eight. Charley went on to Eton, at Miss Coutts's expense, and the others remained at small schools run by clergymen.

Dickens found adolescent boys noisy and irritating, counting the days to the end of their holidays as eagerly as Miss Murdstone, and his sons were despatched to seek their fortunes in the world, often in distant places, quite young. He did not want to force his boys into the wrong mould, and their inclinations, when they had any, were consulted. The diminutive Sydney, who had always longed to be a sailor, went to sea at thirteen. Dickens listened patiently to the stammering, sleep-walking Frank's rapidly changing and contradictory ambitions. But he found it hard to accept that most of his sons had no outstanding intellectual powers or natural talents. Faced with problems about their careers that he could not solve, Dickens's instinct was to remove them from his sight.

Their abrupt ejection from the nest was not a success. Charley, after a spell in the Far East, failed at various businesses and went bankrupt. Walter went into the army. Constantly in debt, he died in India in 1863. Frank was exiled to India, Alfred and Plorn to Australia. Sydney, after an accident at sea, became wildly erratic and irresponsible and died in 1872. Only Harry was a success. He had more support from home than the others, and went to Cambridge instead of into exile (Dickens, though delighted when he won a scholarship, immediately reduced his allowance by the amount of the award). Harry became a judge, was knighted, and lived to be eighty-four.

Though Dickens himself frequently complained of the expenses of a large family, *Little Dorrit* sold even better than *Bleak House*, and after prolonged negotiations he was able to buy the freehold of Gad's Hill Place in March 1856. Since he could not take possession at once the family moved back to Boulogne for the summer, where Dickens planned a new play with Wilkie Collins.

The idea for *The Frozen Deep*, suggested by Sir John Franklin's expedition to the Arctic in 1845, which ended with the death of the entire party, came from Dickens. The play was very much a joint enterprise. The working out of the details of the plot, the first draft and much of the final version were by Collins. Dickens rewrote and added to the dialogue, and took entire charge of the rehearsals.

He and Collins were at their closest at this time, almost inseparable companions. Collins joined the regular staff of *Household Words* in September 1856, and in the same month John Forster, still a bachelor at forty-four, astonished his friends by marrying Eliza Colburn, the rich widow of a publisher. Though Dickens continued to confide in Forster, to whom he had written from Paris the previous winter, 'the skeleton in my domestic closet is becoming a pretty big one',[1] Forster's marriage confirmed his respectable distance from Dickens's turmoil. Only

Collins, the uncensorious friend, appreciated his longing for a bachelor life and his need for entertainment and distraction.

The schoolroom at Tavistock House was torn apart once more in the preparations for *The Frozen Deep*. The cast, which included Georgina Hogarth and Dickens's daughters and older sons, as well as Wilkie Collins and other friends, were drilled relentlessly until Dickens was satisfied. Dickens himself took the central role of Richard Wardour, a villain who redeems himself by saving his rival's life at the expense of his own, basing his portrayal on a performance he had seen given in Paris by the veteran French actor Fréderick Lemaître. Collins played his innocent rival. Four performances were given in January 1857, and were rapturously received by audiences of about ninety on each occasion. The press were invited, and ecstatic reviews appeared in seven London papers. Dickens's acting became the sensation of London. Charley remembered his father's realism in one scene as 'positively alarming – not to say painful'.[2] Collins was also powerfully affected, and Dickens himself admitted that he came close to fainting during one performance.

The fame of the production reached the Queen, who asked Dickens to perform the play at Buckingham Palace. Dickens dared to refuse, explaining that his daughters, as performers, would be in an ambiguous social position at court. Instead, a special performance was staged for the Queen and her guests as one of a number of further perform-ances given at the Gallery of Illustration, Regent Street during the summer. Dickens once more asserted his independence, twice refusing to meet the Queen when she sent for him after the performance, because he was still in costume for the farce that followed the main play. It was a mark of Dickens's extraordinary position not only that he did this, but that the Queen was not offended, and later wrote him a warm, informal letter of appreciation.

Gad's Hill Place was inaugurated with a picnic for Catherine's forty-second birthday on 19 May 1857, and at the beginning of June the family moved there for the summer. Dickens was hard-headed about the property, planning at first to use the house only for summer visits, and to let it at other times to cover costs. There were problems with the water supply, and though Dickens urged his friends to visit, not all the guests were a success. Hans Andersen proved a neurotic and demanding visitor, and Dickens later put a notice in the room he had occupied: 'Hans Andersen slept in this room for five weeks – which seemed to the family AGES.'[3]

Even owning his dream house could not satisfy Dickens. He confessed to Forster that, after all his many improvements to the place, he was not really interested in it. He was no more settled than before, and when Douglas Jerrold, one of his oldest friends, died suddenly in June, Dickens seized the excuse of raising money for Jerrold's family by staging further performances of *The Frozen Deep* in London and Manchester.

Realizing that the voices of the amateur actresses would not be strong enough to carry in the enormous auditorium of the Free Trade Hall in Manchester, Dickens engaged professional actresses for the women's parts. Among these were Mrs Frances Ternan and her two daughters, Maria and Ellen. Maria, who played the young heroine, impressed Dickens by the depth of her emotion at the intensity of his tragic acting, but it was her younger sister Nelly, playing a minor part, who was to become the last great love of his life.

Georgina, Mamie and Kate went to Manchester
with the company, but Catherine did not. She was
very unwell, probably suffering from Dickens's
increasing hostility towards her. He was now openly
telling Forster, 'Poor Catherine and I are not made
for each other . . . she makes me uneasy and unhappy,
. . . I make her so too – and much more so'.[4] He
supposed, despairingly, that they would go on in this
way until death. In her absence, Dickens's infatuation
with Nelly Ternan developed rapidly.

He was forty-five; she was eighteen, the age of
his daughter Kate. Though she had been on the
stage since childhood, the fair, slight girl had an
aura of innocence which aroused all Dickens's
protective instincts. He met her at the moment
when his dissatisfaction with his life was at its
height, and she was associated with the theatre,
which had given him some of the happiest moments
of his existence. But his love for her was not one of
his passing infatuations for a vulnerable young
woman. It was to end his marriage and change the
course of his final years.

When the performances were over and the
company dispersed Dickens, complaining of 'grim

despair and restlessness',[5] suggested to Wilkie Collins that they should take a walking holiday and gather material for a *Household Words* series. The two set off for Cumbria. For the first time Dickens neither wrote to Catherine nor sent his love in his letters to Georgina. He was pursuing, as well as escaping, for he knew that the Ternan sisters would be acting at Doncaster, his ultimate destination. Meanwhile, in a reckless, near-suicidal mood, he insisted on climbing a mountain in rain and mist, without a proper guide. They got lost, Dickens's compass broke, and Collins sprained his ankle so badly that he was unable to walk for days.

Meeting Nelly again at Doncaster confirmed Dickens's obsession. Veiled references to her appeared in *The Lazy Tour of Two Idle Apprentices*, the series of travel pieces written jointly with Collins. In letters to his friends he wrote of his fantasy of rescuing a princess from a tower, and he began to reconstruct the history of his marriage, insisting that he and Catherine had been mismatched from the beginning, ever since Mamie was born. Shortly after returning from Doncaster, he gave orders, without consulting Catherine, for the door between their bedroom and his dressing-room to be blocked up, with a bed for him put in the dressing-room.

He also began to tell everyone that Catherine suffered from bouts of insanity. At least one witness thought that 'Dickens had terrified and depressed her into a dull condition'.[6] His daughter Kate later said that it was her father who was mad at this time. 'This affair brought out all that was worst – all that was weakest in him. He did not care a damn what happened to any of us. Nothing could surpass the misery and unhappiness of our home.'[7]

In this condition Dickens was unable to write anything substantial, and revived the idea of doing public readings from his works. He had been doing these occasionally for years to raise money for charity; now he proposed a tour of thirty-five to forty readings to make money for himself – and, though he did not acknowledge this, to help Nelly and her family. Miss Coutts, who had always disliked Dickens's theatricals, was firmly against the idea. Forster was equally disapproving, feeling it was undignified, would take Dickens away from any possibility of reviving his family life, and would be too exhausting. Dickens claimed Forster's objections were irrational, and insisted, 'I should rust, break, and die, if I spared myself. Much better to die, doing.'[8]

He began his first series of readings in April 1858. A month later, Catherine, worn down by Dickens's behaviour, agreed to move out of her home and sign a settlement ending their marriage. Miss Coutts immediately offered her shelter. Catherine was grateful, but chose to move to a house of her own in Gloucester Crescent, Regent's Park, with an allowance of £600 a year. By agreement with Dickens her eldest son Charley went with her, but Dickens kept all the other children, justifying this by claiming, quite unreasonably, that Catherine had always been a useless mother whose children disliked and feared her.

Georgina also stayed with Dickens. He had now convinced himself that Georgina was the only effective mother the children had ever had. Georgina, though she had attempted to keep the marriage going, thought Dickens could do no wrong. Inevitably, rumours about their relationship started flying round London. Thackeray, told that Dickens was having an affair with his sister-in-law, denied it, but his correction – that the affair was with an actress

– infuriated Dickens further, and led to a quarrel which lasted until shortly before Thackeray's death.

Dickens frantically asserted his innocence of all charges. Believing that Catherine's mother and youngest sister Helen were responsible for some of the scandal, he forced them, on the threat of withdrawing his settlement on Catherine, to sign a statement upholding his moral character, and forbade his children to see them. He wrote a letter justifying his behaviour to Arthur Smith, the manager of his reading tours, authorizing him to use it as he saw fit. This later found its way into the papers, and became known as 'the violated letter' though it is unclear who was responsible for its publication. He also drew up a statement, so vaguely worded as to bewilder all but his intimates, which he published in *Household Words* and sent to the newspapers to be copied. When Mark Lemon, the old friend who had acted for Catherine over the settlement, refused to publish it in *Punch*, Dickens quarrelled with him fiercely. He also attacked Bradbury & Evans, who published both *Punch* and *Household Words*, for upholding Lemon's decision. The rift resulted in Dickens reverting to his earlier publishers, Chapman & Hall, and closing down *Household Words*.

Less than two years after first meeting Ellen Ternan, Dickens had ended his marriage, destroyed his magazine, fallen out with some of his closest friends, and seriously compromised his position in English society. Astonishingly, in spite of adverse comments in the newspapers, he kept his public. A second reading tour throughout Britain from the autumn of 1858 to January 1859 was an over-whelming success, personally and financially.

Dickens was euphoric. As soon as the tour ended he energetically set about planning another magazine. From a number of titles (Forster talked him out of *Household Harmony*) he finally decided on *All the Year Round*, and publication began at the end of April. *All the Year Round* proved even more successful than *Household Words*, partly owing to the weekly serialization of a popular novel, the first his own *A Tale of Two Cities*. He took the bold decision to publish the story simultaneously in monthly numbers, in order to 'give me my old standing with my old public'.[9] *A Tale of Two Cities* was followed by Wilkie Collins's equally successful *The Woman in White*.

A Tale of Two Cities was Dickens's first historical fiction since the early *Barnaby Rudge*. Strongly influenced by Carlyle's best-selling *History of the French Revolution* of 1837, it reflected the English mixture of sympathy, fascination and horror with the events of the Revolution and the Terror. The subject allowed him to hammer home the dangers of keeping the working class oppressed and uneducated, playing on fears aroused by the Chartist Movement of the 1840s, and emphasizing the need for parliamentary reform. It also provided an emotionally charged setting for his most romantic novel, a story of love and self-sacrifice.

The inspiration for Sidney Carton, the flawed hero redeemed by his voluntary death, had come to Dickens as he lay acting the death of a similar character in *The Frozen Deep*, wept over by Maria Ternan. He was, he confessed, much attached to Carton, and he gave Lucie Manette, the girl Carton loves and relinquishes, Nelly Ternan's looks. But the self-sacrificial role was strictly fictional. He may have agonized over what was best for Nelly, but he was not going to give her up. It was Catherine, his children, and Nelly herself who were sacrificed.

He insisted that his relationship with Nelly was platonic, telling his children that it was their mother's jealous nature that made her incapable of believing this. Nelly and he may not yet have been lovers, so that he could claim in the 'violated letter' she was 'a young lady . . . innocent and pure, and as good as my own dear daughters'.[10] He behaved as though the separation were Catherine's fault. 'I want to forgive her and forget her,' he wrote.[11] Though, as he often pointed out, he was financially generous to her, he never saw her again. When their son Walter died in India Dickens refused to meet her and did not write to her; the sad details had to be conveyed through Georgina. Catherine was not asked to the wedding of her daughter Kate.

For the rest of her life Catherine lived a quiet, uncomplaining life of virtual widowhood in her house in Gloucester Crescent, seeing her children when she could, and writing to them affectionately when they were apart – the children were permitted to see their mother, but not encouraged to do so. Kate, who later became her champion, did not see her regularly until she herself married. Kate blamed herself and her siblings for being too much under their father's influence, but his powerful personality was difficult to resist.

FINAL YEARS, 1859–70

Dickens saw Nelly Ternan often, but he led his double life with great discretion. The lease of a house in Ampthill Square, not far from Tavistock House, was bought for her, where she lived at first with her mother and sisters – clearly Dickens had won her mother's consent to the relationship. In 1859 Nelly gave up the stage altogether. Dickens, preferring her to be out of the public eye, must have been supporting her. He was also helping her sisters, repeatedly recommending Maria to theatrical managers. He paid for Fanny to study singing in Florence for a year, and later introduced her to the widowed Tom Trollope, brother of the novelist Anthony, as a suitable governess for his daughter. Fanny married her employer in 1866, and herself later became a successful novelist.

Nelly was introduced to Dickens's daughters and Georgina, and Mamie and Georgina befriended her. Kate, more detached and wary, later said that Nelly was clever, and took pains to educate herself to be a companion to Dickens. He needed distraction. He had aged under the strain of the last few years, and frequently complained of being unwell. Though he enjoyed the reading tours, he found them exhausting. His personal charities continued, and he did much to support the Great Ormond Street Children's Hospital, but he cut down the range of his public commitments. He gradually gave up his association with Urania Cottage. Without Dickens's dynamism the project soon folded, and though his friendship with Miss Coutts continued, their relationship was markedly less close after the separation. Dickens did not appreciate her continued efforts to bring about a reconciliation with Catherine.

Dickens's family continued to burden him. His brothers still demanded money, and his refusal to lend Frederick £30 in 1857 brought an angry accusation that he was 'cold and unfeeling';[1] Frederick woundingly contrasted Dickens's public reputation for tolerance with the inflexibility of his private behaviour. The marriages of both Frederick and Augustus broke up, and his other brother Alfred died in 1860, leaving a widow and children for Dickens to support. 'I never had anything left to me but relations,' he commented ruefully.[2] His mother lingered on until 1863, senile, but still game: to Dickens's amusement 'she plucked up a spirit and asked me for "a pound"'.[3] Augustus died in 1866. When Frederick died in 1868 Dickens thought his had been a wasted life, but was comfortably selective when remembering him. 'I do not recollect, thank God, that a hard word was passed between us.'[4] His sister Letitia's husband Henry Austin died in 1861, also leaving debts. Austin, a civil engineer, had been indispensable to Dickens in advising and collaborating with him on public health campaigns, and supervising the alterations and improvements made to his various houses. However, Dickens was more distressed by the death in the same year of his tour manager, Arthur Smith. His replacement, George Dolby, though enthusiastic and willing, proved less efficient.

In August 1860 Dickens made the decision to live permanently at Gad's Hill. He sold Tavistock House, the family home since 1851, keeping in London only a bachelor flat over the offices of *All the Year Round*. As if to symbolize the ending of the married phase of his life, he made a huge bonfire at Gad's Hill, on which he burned the letters and papers of the past twenty years. He said he wished he could have got hold of every letter he had ever written, to add them to the pyre. From then onwards he destroyed every personal letter he received.

Some versions of his past, autobiographical musings on his childhood and youth, appeared in *The Uncommercial Traveller* essays which appeared in *All the Year Round* from January 1860. He wrote of early love and despair, but never of his marriage. The essays included some of his best mature social journalism, though the reader can sometimes detect a hardening of attitudes. He was still nominally radical, and in favour of the 1867 Reform Bill on the grounds that an enlarged electorate could hardly do worse than the existing one. But in his property-owning middle age he came to feel that there was an irredeemable element in society. The universal education for which he had always campaigned was supposed to make the poor self-reliant, virtuous and industrious citizens. But education, as he could see from his own children's failures, was not a complete answer. Though he still deplored public executions, capital punishment now seemed the only appropriate punishment for murderers. He fiercely attacked any defenders of the Indian mutineers or the plantation workers involved in the Jamaican insurrection of 1865 (put down with great brutality by Governor Eyre). Though against slavery, he had all the usual prejudices of the time against people of a different colour.

Dickens cared, with tactful sympathy, for those in any trouble whom he knew personally, such as his old servants. But several large, fierce dogs were kept at Gad's Hill to discourage tramps and intruders, and the gardener carried a gun. Dickens, who had, more than anyone, given names and faces to the deprived, now lapsed at times into the unthinking prejudices of his contemporaries.

He was clearly not happy in the last years of his life. He seemed to have found, like Pip, that his 'great expectations' had turned to ashes. Some particular but unspecified anxiety haunted him in 1862 and 1863, years in which he spent much time in France – this was possibly Nelly's pregnancy, followed by the death of her child. He was still restless and unsatisfied, though his eager appetite for life had markedly diminished. In a letter to Forster, perhaps to explain his increased reticence, he related his current state of mind to his childhood. 'The never to be forgotten misery of that old time, bred a certain shrinking sensitiveness . . . that I have found come back in the never to be forgotten misery of this later time.'[5] This sense of being haunted by the past continued to reverberate in Dickens's fiction. In *A Tale of Two Cities*, as in *Little Dorrit*, he imagined a middle-aged man returning, at a moment of stress, to the habits and circumstances of a time of earlier trauma.

He was also distressed to see his older children making, as he felt, disastrous mistakes about marriage. Kate, who found the situation at home intolerable, married Charles Collins in July 1860. Dickens, who was irritated by his ineffectual son-in-law, felt guiltily responsible for Kate leaving home. Charles, very different from his hedonistic brother Wilkie, was a depressed, gentle character, an artist associated with the beginnings of the Pre-Raphaelite Movement, who was often ill. He had given up painting, which he found stressful, and now made a precarious living from journalism. Kate was fond of Charles, but, she later confessed, was not in love with him: Dickens felt she was ruining her life. Later, when Kate was thinking of asking for a separation from her husband, who was rumoured to be impotent, Dickens would not allow her to do so, presumably fearing the publicity. Mamie, said to be in love with a married man, never married. He fiercely opposed Charley's marriage to the daughter of his 'enemy' Frederick Evans. He did not attend the ceremony, and even asked Charley's godfather, Thomas Beard, not to go to the reception in Evans's house. A reconciliation took place when Charley's first child was born, and though his grandchildren were never allowed to call him 'grandfather', he transferred to them his habitual delight in babies and toddlers.

Dickens's next novel, *Great Expectations*, indirectly revealed his consciousness of his own personal failures. The novel, serialized in *All the Year Round* during 1861, proved that his creativity had not only survived, but deepened. Pip, perhaps the most interesting of Dickens's young heroes, makes a painful journey from unthinking selfishness and snobbery to self-awareness, redeemed partly through his tormented love for Estella, partly through his acceptance of the true facts of his past. Dickens originally planned an unhappy ending to the novel, with Pip and Estella parting for ever. He was persuaded by Bulwer-Lytton to change it.

There was to be no happy ending for him. He longed for Catherine's death – he frankly admitted it – so that he might marry Nelly; but she was to survive him by nine years. Meanwhile his convoluted double life continued. On the surface, life at Gad's Hill went on as usual. The house was constantly altered and improved: a conservatory was added, and a miniature Swiss chalet was erected in the garden, the upper storey providing an idyllic summer writing-room among the tree-tops. The flower-beds blazed with scarlet geraniums, his favourite flower. There were guests; family life was to some extent reconstructed under Georgina's watchful supervision. But Dickens vanished for days or weeks at a time, on visits to France or to appear under the alias 'Charles Tringham' at houses in Slough and Peckham where Nelly was lodging. It was a dangerous game: on one occasion he was seen on a cross-Channel steamer with Nelly. She sometimes made discreet visits to Gad's Hill and was present in the audience at his readings, but it was a sad and lonely life for a young woman, relieved chiefly by visits to her married sisters.

In *Our Mutual Friend*, Dickens's last completed novel, the hard and difficult life of Lizzie Hexam, the working-class heroine who narrowly escapes ruin by the young man who eventually marries her, may owe something to Dickens's appreciation of Nelly's situation. But Lizzie's story, and the powerful character of her other lover, the homicidal Bradley Headstone, is confined to a sub-plot. It is the complicated history of John Harmon, a man who voluntarily gives up his identity and his inheritance to spy on the girl he was supposed to marry, in order to discover her real character, that takes centre stage.

Our Mutual Friend, serialized in *All the Year Round* during 1864 and 1865, was nearing completion when Dickens, Nelly and her mother were involved in a horrific railway crash at Staplehurst, between Dover and London, on their return from a visit to France. A bridge collapsed and the train went off the rails, killing and badly injuring numbers of travellers. Nelly was slightly hurt. Dickens was untouched, and spent hours helping heroically with the injured and dying. He suffered greatly from reaction later, and for years hated travelling in trains or carriages. It was a serious consideration on his second visit to the United States.

Dickens had many times been asked to read in America, and the invitation was renewed in 1866. Both Wills and Forster were against it, feeling the strain would be too great. Dickens's doctor had diagnosed degeneration of his heart a few months earlier, and prescribed digitalis. Dickens himself was initially reluctant, afraid that the unpopularity aroused after his 1842 trip might still linger. Also, he did not want to leave Nelly for so long. However, he was promised a minimum of £10,000, and the prospect of making so much money – in the event he made nearly twice as much – finally proved irresistible. After a grand farewell banquet in his honour he set sail in November 1867.

Cryptic entries in a secret diary for 1867, which survived the general destruction of Dickens's papers only because it was lost or stolen in America, strongly suggest that in April 1867 Nelly gave birth to a child which died six days later. Certainly Nelly was ill that month. By the time Dickens left for America she had recovered, and he hoped she might be able to join him there. He arranged to send a coded telegram via Wills: 'All well' meant she should come; 'Safe and well' that she should not.[6] On his arrival at Boston he seems to have confided in his American publisher, James Fields, and his wife Annie, who became an adoring admirer. Three days later he sent the negative message. He badly missed Nelly throughout the trip, and his letters to Wills, his channel of communication with her, were full of his love and longing.

Dickens found America had changed since his earlier tour, and, he decided, for the better. People were as enthusiastic as ever, and hundreds were turned away from every reading, but they were more considerate, and respectful of his privacy. Those who knew him from 1842 noticed how much he had altered. The eager, active, and iconoclastic dandy of twenty-five years earlier had gone; he was ageing, and visibly ill. He suffered from a severe cold which left him with troublesome catarrh, and his left foot was often so swollen that he could not get his boot on. Normally abstemious, he was able to eat and drink even less than usual as the tour progressed. By the end he was eating almost no solid food, existing on raw eggs beaten up in brandy. He strictly limited his social engagements, and saved his energy for the readings. It is hardly surprising that the young Henry James, overwhelmed by his first meeting with the master, should comment on his 'inscrutable mask'.[7] Emerson's comment was more searching. He described Dickens's genius as 'a fearful locomotive to which he is bound and can never be free from it or set at rest. . . . He is too consummate an artist to have a thread of nature left. He daunts me! I have not the key.'[8]

Though Dickens enjoyed re-encountering many American friends, and making new ones, the readings and the travelling involved exhausted him. He slept badly, and was often depressed. The readings became as much a torment to be endured as a direct communication with his readers, and he decided that he would do only one more reading tour in England. With the money earned in America, he had made £33,000 from the readings in the years 1866–8.

He should have been able to relax; but there were problems waiting for him in London. Wills, on whom he had relied for so many years, had a bad fall from his horse while Dickens was in America, and was unable to work for months. Dickens found a mass of business to attend to at the magazine offices. He appointed his son Charley, bankrupt and with a family to support, to the staff, but he was hardly an effective substitute for Wills.

The parting from Plorn, despatched in tears to Australia in September, was almost unbearably painful. Plorn carried with him a letter of admonition for his lack of 'set, steady, constant purpose'[9] – hardly surprising at sixteen. Harry, off to Cambridge a few weeks later, was exhorted to keep out of debt and stop depending on his father as soon as possible. Only the unmarried, adoring Mamie still remained at home to keep Georgina in countenance.

Dickens was now eager to end the readings, though he expected to miss them. Determined to make the last series the best, he devised a new reading based on the murder of Nancy by Sikes in *Oliver Twist*. It was to become the most memorable and celebrated of all, but it was widely credited with precipitating his death. To test whether it was too horrific for the public to stomach, he tried it out on a group of friends. The verdict was almost unanimous;

he should not do it. The artistic effect was overwhelming, but the danger to his health too great.

Nevertheless Dickens was determined to include it, and 'Sikes and Nancy' became the keystone of the final readings of 1868–70. Though Dickens was by now having problems with his speech, mispronouncing the names of his characters, and suffering defects of vision, as well as continued pain in his foot, he 'murdered Nancy' ten times in one week in 1869. Only when he suffered a minor stroke in April did he accept his doctor's insistence that he must give up the tour. He had given 72 out of 100 planned readings.

Though he claimed that he had made a complete recovery, Dickens made a new will in May 1869. It included a legacy of £1,000 to Nelly Ternan, continued provision for Catherine during her lifetime, and for Mamie while she remained unmarried. Forster became his literary executor, and Georgina was left £8,000 and most of his personal belongings.

In August he began a new novel, *The Mystery of Edwin Drood*. A dark story of addiction, obsession and murder, it owed much to the example of Wilkie Collins. His public had not deserted him in the long interval since *Our Mutual Friend*, and the first number sold 50,000 copies. Some of Dickens's old enthusiasm returned as he wrote, and he managed to produce instalments of the novel while giving a farewell series of twelve readings in London. He read for the last time in March, a highly emotional occasion for both Dickens and his audience, choosing to end with *A Christmas Carol*. In the same month he finally met Queen Victoria, at her request, in a private audience at Buckingham Palace which both seemed to enjoy.

His favourite child Kate visited him at Gad's Hill on 5 June to ask his advice about going on the stage. He begged her not to, telling her she was clever enough to do something else. She found him much changed, and noticed that he spoke as though his life was over, warning her he might not live to finish *Edwin Drood*. They talked far into the night, and he told her much she had not known about his life, wishing he had been a better father and a better man.

Three days later, at dinner with Georgina, Dickens suffered a paralytic stroke. The doctor was called, but there was nothing to be done. Mamie, Kate, Charley, and Nelly Ternan were summoned. Dickens was laid on the dining room sofa, and died the next day without regaining consciousness.

Dickens, who deplored the elaborate flummery of Victorian funerals, had stipulated a simple ceremony. He wanted to be buried in Rochester, under the wall of the castle, but his last gesture against ostentation was only partly successful. The funeral was kept private, with only family and close friends attending, but an obscure grave was not thought suitable for the literary hero of his age: he belonged to the nation, and must lie with the great and the good in Poet's Corner, Westminster Abbey. 'The Inimitable Boz' was indisputably a great writer. He had tried to be a good man. Only with those closest to him, perhaps, had he failed.

N O T E S

References to the works of Charles Dickens are taken from *The Oxford Illustrated Dickens*, Oxford, Oxford University Press, 1987.

INTRODUCTION

1. Philip Collins (ed.), *Dickens: The Critical Heritage* (London, Routledge & Kegan Paul, 1971), pp. xvi–xvii.
2. Charles Dickens, *The Collected Letters of Charles Dickens*, ed. Madeline House, Graham Storey, Kathleen Tillotson *et al.* (12 vols, Oxford, The Clarendon Press, 1965–2002) (hereinafter referred to as *Letters*) vol. 2, p. 418.

CHAPTER ONE

1. Charles Dickens, *David Copperfield*, p. 163.
2. Charles Dickens, *The Uncommercial Traveller*, 'Nurse's Stories', p. 150.
3. Dickens, *The Uncommercial Traveller*, 'Dullborough Town', p. 120.
4. John Forster, *The Life of Charles Dickens*, J.W.T. Ley (ed.) (London, Cecil Palmer, 1928), p. 47.
5. Dickens, *David Copperfield*, p. 53.
6. Dickens, 'Dullborough Town', p. 116.

7. Forster, *The Life of Charles Dickens*, p. 47.
8. Ibid., p. 10.
9. Ibid., p. 26.
10. Ibid., p. 27.
11. Ibid., p. 35.
12. *Letters*, vol. 6, p. 635.
13. Forster, *The Life of Charles Dickens*, p. 35.
14. Philip Collins (ed.), *Dickens: Interviews and Recollections* (2 vols, London, Macmillan, 1981), vol. 1, p. 134.

CHAPTER TWO

1. Charles Dickens, *Pickwick Papers*, 1845, Preface.
2. *Letters*, vol. 3, p. 191.
3. Collins, *Interviews*, vol. 1, p. 62.
4. William Makepeace Thackeray, *Letters and Private Papers*, Gordon Ray (ed.) (4 vols, London, The Clarendon Press, 1945), vol. 2, p. 110.
5. Collins, *Interviews*, vol. 1, p. 39.
6. *Letters*, vol. 2, p. 180.
7. Ibid., p. 171.
8. Ibid., p. 410.
9. *Letters*, vol. 3, p. 575.

CHAPTER THREE

1. *Letters*, vol. 3, p. 34.
2. Collins, *Interviews*, vol. 1, p. 53.
3. Charles Dickens, *American Notes*, p. 99.
4. *Letters*, vol. 3, p. 427.
5. Ibid., p. 176.
6. Ibid., p. 563.
7. Charles Dickens, *Uncollected Writings from Household Words*, Harry Stone (ed.) (2 vols, London, Allen Lane, The Penguin Press, 1969), vol. 1, p. 193–4.
8. *Letters*, vol. 3, p. 590.
9. *Letters*, vol. 4, p. 200.
10. Ibid., p. 208.

11. *Letters*, vol. 7, p. 224.

12. *Letters*, vol. 5, pp. 216, 217.

13. Ibid., p. 478.

14. Ibid., p. 154n.

15. Collins, *Interviews*, vol. 1, p. 89.

16. *Letters*, vol. 3, p. 483.

17. *Letters*, vol. 4, p. 267; vol. 6, p. 158; Forster, *The Life of Charles Dickens*, p. 857.

18. Forster, *The Life of Charles Dickens*, p. 604.

19. Ibid., p. 613.

20. *Letters*, vol. 5, p. 19.

Chapter Four

1. William Thackeray, *Letters and Private Papers*, vol. 2, p. 266.

2. Forster, *The Life of Charles Dickens*, p. 427.

3. *Letters*, vol. 6, pp. 25, 244.

4. Dickens, *David Copperfield*, Preface.

5. *Letters*, vol. 6, p. viii.

6. *Household Words*, vol. 1, p. 1.

7. *Letters*, vol. 6, p. 314.

8. Dickens, *Bleak House*, Chapter 16, p. 219.

9. Ibid., Chapter 47, p. 649.

10. *Letters*, vol. 7, p. 173.

11. Ibid., p. 282.

12. Collins, *Critical Heritage*, p. 300.

13. Ibid., p. 314.

14. *Letters*, vol. 7, p. 543.

15. Ibid., p. 245.

16. Ibid., p. 713.

Chapter Five

1. *Letters*, vol. 8, p. 89.

2. Collins, *Interviews*, vol. 1, p. 134.

3. Edgar Johnson, *Charles Dickens: His Tragedy and Triumph* (Harmondsworth, Penguin Books, 1986), p. 444.

4. Forster, *The Life of Charles Dickens*, p. 640.

5. *Letters*, vol. 8, p. 423.

6. Ibid., p. 471n.

7. Collins, *Interviews*, vol. 1, p. 152.

8. *Letters*, vol. 8, p. 464.

9. *Letters*, vol. 8, p. 35.

10. Michael Slater, *Dickens and Women* (London, J.M. Dent & Sons, 1983), p. 374.

11. *Letters*, vol. 8, p. 632.

CHAPTER SIX

1. *Letters*, vol. 8, p. 277.

2. *Letters*, vol. 8, p. 287.

3. *The Pilgrim Edition of the Letters of Charles Dickens*, vol. 8, p. 277n.

4. *Letters*, vol. 12, p. 207.

5. *Letters*, vol. 10, p. 98.

6. Claire Tomalin, *The Invisible Woman* (London, Viking, 1990), p. 180.

7. Collins, *Interviews*, vol. 2, p. 297.

8. Ibid., vol. 2, p. 318–19.

9. *Letters*, vol. 12, p. 187.

B I B L I O G R A P H Y

The place of publication is London unless otherwise stated.

Dickens, Charles, Collected Works

The Oxford Illustrated Dickens Oxford, Oxford University Press, 1987 edition

Dickens, Charles, Letters and Miscellaneous Writings

Slater, Michael (ed.), *Dickens's Journalism* vols 1–4, J.M. Dent, 1994–2000

House, Madeline, Storey, Graham, Tillotson, Kathleen, (general editors), *The Collected Letters of Charles Dickens*, 12 vols, Oxford, The Clarendon Press, 1965–2002

Matz, B.W. (ed.), *Miscellaneous Papers*, Chapman & Hall, 1914

Shepherd, R.H. (ed.), *The Plays and Poems of Charles Dickens*, 2 vols, W.H. Allen, 1885

Fielding, K.J. (ed.), *The Speeches of Charles Dickens*, Oxford, The
   Clarendon Press, 1960

Stone, Harry (ed.), *Charles Dickens' Uncollected Writings from
   Household Words*, 2 vols, London, Allen Lane, The Penguin
   Press, 1969

Reference Works

Bentley, Nicolas, Burgis, Nina, Slater, Michael, *The Dickens
   Index*, Oxford, Oxford University Press, 1988

Collins, Philip, *Dickens: The Critical Heritage*, Routledge & Kegan
   Paul, 1971

———. *Dickens: Interviews and Recollections*, Macmillan, 1981

Page, Norman, *A Dickens Chronology*, Macmillan, 1988

Biographies

Ackroyd, Peter, *Dickens*, Guild Publishing, 1990

Forster, John, *The Life of Charles Dickens*, J.W.T. Ley (ed.), Cecil
   Palmer, 1928

Johnson, Edgar, *Charles Dickens: His Tragedy and Triumph* (revised
   edition), Harmondsworth, Penguin Books, 1986

Kaplan, Fred, *Dickens: A Biography*, Hodder & Stoughton, 1988

MacKenzie, Norman and Jeanne, *Dickens: A Life*, Oxford,
   Oxford University Press, 1979

Tomalin, Claire, *The Invisible Woman: The Story of Nelly Ternan and
   Charles Dickens*, Viking, 1990

Wilson, Angus, *The World of Charles Dickens*, Secker & Warburg, 1970

B i b l i o g r a p h y

Criticism and Commentary

Butt, John, and Kathleen Tillotson, *Dickens at Work*, Methuen, 1968

Carey, John, *The Violent Effigy: A Study of Dickens' Imagination*, Faber & Faber, 1973

Collins, Philip, *Dickens and Crime*, Macmillan, 1994

——. *Dickens and Education*, Macmillan, 1965

Grant, Allan, *A Preface to Dickens*, Longman, 1984

Patten, Robert L., *Charles Dickens and his Publishers*, Oxford, Oxford University Press, 1978

Slater, Michael, *Dickens and Women*, J.M. Dent, 1983

Smith, Grahame, *Charles Dickens: A Literary Life*, Macmillan, 1996

Welsh, Alexander, *The City of Dickens*, Oxford, The Clarendon Press, 1971

Literary and Historical Background

Davies, James A., *John Forster: A Literary Life*, Leicester, Leicester University Press, 1983

Flint, Kate (ed.), *The Victorian Novelist: Social Problems and Social Change*, New York, Croom Helm in association with Methuen, 1987

Harvey, John, *Victorian Novelists and their Illustrators*, Sidgwick & Jackson, 1970

Houghton, Walter, *The Victorian Frame of Mind: 1830–1870*, New Haven, Yale University Press, 1970

Peters, Catherine, *The King of Inventors: A Life of Wilkie Collins*, Minerva Press, 1992

Tillotson, Kathleen, *Novels of the Eighteen Forties*, Oxford, Oxford University Press, 1985

I N D E X

I n d e x

Smith, Arthur, 83, 89

Ternan, Ellen (Nelly), 78, 79, 80, 81,
    84, 85, 87, 92, 94, 95, 96–7,
    100, 101
Ternan, Frances (Fanny), 87, 88, 95
Ternan, Mrs Frances, 78, 87, 95
Ternan, Maria, 78, 81, 85, 87, 95

Thackeray, William Makepeace, 21, 30,
    31, 52, 82
Weller, Christiana, 49–50
Weller, Mary, 5, 22
Wills, William Henry, 57, 58, 59, 60,
    96, 97, 98

Victoria, Queen, 62, 77, 101